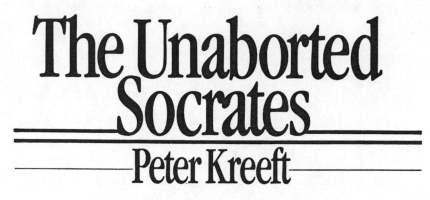

The Unaborted Socrates

Peter Kreeft

A dramatic debate on the issues
surrounding abortion.

InterVarsity Press
Downers Grove
Illinois 60515

InterVarsity Press is the book-publishing division of Inter-Varsity Christian Fellowship, a student movement active on campus at hundreds of universities, colleges and schools of nursing. For information about local and regional activities, write IVCF, 233 Langdon St., Madison, WI 53703.

Distributed in Canada through InterVarsity Press, 860 Denison St., Unit 3, Markham, Ontario L3R 4H1, Canada.

Cover illustration: Joe DeVelasco

ISBN 0-87784-810-6

Printed in the United States of America

Library of Congress Cataloging in Publication Data

Kreeft, Peter.
   The unaborted Socrates.

   1. Abortion.   2. Socrates.   I. Title.
HQ767.K73   1983   179'.76   83-8430
ISBN 0-87784-810-6

17	16	15	14	13	12	11	10	9	8	7	6	5	4	3	2	1
96	95	94	93	92	91	90	89	88	87	86	85	84	83			

For Balduin and Stephen Schwarz,
who mightily refute Nietzsche's
divorce between Truth and Life

CONTENTS

Acknowledgments

Copious thanks belong to Joan Guest, Kathryn Lindskoog,
the Rev. Eugene Peterson, Stephen Evans,
Clifton Orlebeke, Kirk Kilpatrick, Fr. Ronald Tacelli,
James Sire (the Platonic ideal of an editor) and most
especially Stephen Schwarz for reading the manuscript and
making excellent suggestions, not all of which
I followed (so of course any quarrel any reader has with
any sin of omission or commission here is with me,
not with these good counselors).

DIALOG ONE
SOCRATES IN AN ABORTION CLINIC

time: *the present*
place: *a hospital in Athens*

dramatis personae:
Socrates
Dr. Rex Herrod, abortionist

Socrates: Where are we?

Dr. Herrod: We? I know perfectly well where *I* am, but you appear disoriented, Sir.

Socrates: Appearances may be deceiving. Perhaps it is the one who seems to know, who really does not know.

Herrod: You're a strange sort of person. Why do you speak classical Greek?

Socrates: I speak my native tongue.

Herrod: What is your native city?

Socrates: Athens.

Herrod: Here? You look like one who has come from afar.

Socrates: Indeed I have. But not far in space.

Herrod: Oh. I . . . see.

Socrates: Do you?

Herrod: Perhaps you want the psychiatric ward?

Socrates: No. I have been sent *here.*

Herrod: Are you a doctor?

Socrates: Of a sort.

Herrod: What sort? I think you must be in the wrong place.

Socrates: This is an abortion clinic, is it not?

Herrod: Why, yes. Do you perform abortions?

Socrates: Of a sort. I abort thoughts.

Herrod: Thoughts?

Socrates: Yes. Fallacies. Inconsistencies. Ignorance. I terminate defective intellectual pregnancies.

Herrod: Oh. Is *that* all?

Socrates: No, that is not all. I am an intellectual ob-stetrician—a midwife of thoughts, you might say.

Herrod: A . . . midwife of thoughts?

Socrates: Yes. Logical thoughts. Consistencies.

Herrod: You sound like a lunatic to me. What is that

strange white gown you're wearing?

Socrates: My daily clothes. What is that strange white gown *you're* wearing?

Herrod: I'm a doctor—Dr. Rex Herrod. But you look like a cross between a doctor and a ghost.

Socrates: I am both, in a way.

Herrod: Well, I don't believe you are a doctor, and I don't believe in ghosts.

Socrates: That makes no difference. I am here.

Herrod: What do you want?

Socrates: Only some conversation. Perhaps you would indulge my curiosity and tell me about your work here.

Herrod: Hmmm . . . why don't you sit down here in this comfortable chair and I'll get some coffee.

Socrates: You mean this uncomfortable chair? All right, but I do not want any coffee.

Herrod: Can I get you anything to eat?

Socrates: Yes. Some thoughts, if you please.

Herrod: You eat thoughts?

Socrates: Certainly. To begin with an appetizer, what are you doing here?

Herrod: I know perfectly well what *I'm* doing here. The question is, what are *you* doing here?

Socrates: What I'm doing here is asking you questions about what you're doing here. If you "know perfectly well," you should have no trouble answering now, should you?

Herrod: You are a strange one, whoever you are. All right, I'll play your little game if you wish. I perform abortions here.

Socrates: You sound defensive.

Herrod: Surely you realize my work is controversial.

Socrates: Indeed I do. Some think your work is good

and some think it is evil.

Herrod: It is neither. It is neutral. It is not a moral issue, but a medical issue.

Socrates: You are paid for this work, are you not?

Herrod: Of course.

Socrates: Are people paid for things that help or for things that harm or for things that neither help nor harm?

Herrod: Things that help, surely. They are called services.

Socrates: And what helps is good, is it not? Just as what harms is evil?

Herrod: Yes.

Socrates: Then this service of yours must be good, since people pay you for it, and they pay only for services that help, and what helps is good.

Herrod: Fine. Let it be as you say. My service is good, if you put it that way.

Socrates: No, it is *you* who put it that way.

Herrod: What if I do?

Socrates: Then your work is not neutral, as you said before, but either good or evil. You believe your work is good, but others believe it is evil. Why do they believe that? And how do you defend yourself against their arguments?

Herrod: Two very large questions indeed. You're asking for the two sides of the abortion controversy.

Socrates: In a nutshell, as you would say.

Herrod: Why are you doing this?

*The
Socratic
service:
helping
people know
what they're
doing*

Socrates: I too perform a service. I help people know what they are doing.

Herrod: I know perfectly well what I'm doing.

Socrates: That remains to be seen.

Herrod: I see. You're playing Socrates.

Socrates: No. Not *playing.*

Herrod: I told you I don't believe in ghosts. But as you say, it makes no difference. You are here. I shall even call you Socrates if you like.

Socrates: Thank you—though you give me only what is mine. May we begin then?

Herrod: All right. It will be amusing for you and may be instructive for me.

Socrates: I think rather vice versa: it is you who are only amusing yourself by playing a game with me. I, on the other hand, really want to know, to be instructed by you in this matter. If you are in the business of performing services, perhaps you can perform one for me which is literally priceless; and it is only fitting that I cannot pay you for it. That is the service of teaching me.

Herrod: Let it be as you say.

Socrates: Teach me then. Why is your work good?

Herrod: I thought you just proved it was good with that little argument of yours.

Socrates: Not mine; ours. Did you not agree to it?

Herrod: Ours, then. What was wrong with the argument?

Socrates: For one thing, it lacked demonstrative force. It did not tell the cause, the real reason for its conclusion. It argued from the effect rather than from the cause. So please tell me now: why is your work good, Dr. Herrod?

Herrod: Let my opponents tell me why it is *not* good, if you please. The onus of proof is on them, not on me. A suspect should be presumed innocent until proved guilty, and a deed should be presumed good or at least neutral, until proved evil. The "liberal presumption" is on my side.

The "liberal presumption": the onus of proof is on the anti-abortionist

Socrates: Already we seem to have a major shift of ground in our battle. You seem to have assumed the stronger position at the start. What attack, then, do your opponents use to try to overcome this "liberal presumption"? Surely it must be a strong argument to overcome such a strong presumption of innocence.

Herrod: No, Socrates, it is a ridiculously weak one. It uses an emotional term to befuddle the issue.

Socrates: And what term is that?

Is abortion murder?

Herrod: Murder. They say abortion is murder. So they're calling me a murderer. Worse, they're calling millions of pregnant women murderers.

Socrates: Perhaps we should begin by distinguishing two questions which your opponents, it seems, fail to distinguish, if they really call all women who have abortions murderers.

Herrod: Well, they don't exactly say that. But that is certainly the logical implication: if abortion is murder, then an abortionist is a murderer.

Socrates: In an objective sense, perhaps, but not necessarily in a subjective sense. That is the distinction I would like to make between the two questions. The question I would like to discuss with you is this: what is abortion—the act itself? Is it murder or not? That question, it seems to me, might be decided, if we are both careful and fortunate in our reasoning. But the other question of the personal guilt of an individual, the question of responsibility and blame, seems to me a much more complex question. Even if abortion *were* murder, it may be that (as some would say) it is "society's fault" or the fault of bad philosophy. A pregnant woman who comes to you does not come with the clear intent to commit murder, does she?

Distinguishing two questions: the act and the intention

Herrod: Certainly not. It's not like a criminal coming

to a hired assassin. Abortion is not like assassination.

Socrates: I do not know *that* yet. You see, that is my first question: what is abortion? I think it would take a knowledge more than human to read the heart and the intention, but it does not take more than human reason to define the act. So since we are both rational human beings, let us embark on that task now, if you please.

Herrod: All right.

Socrates: Your opponents claim that abortion is murder, and you claim that it is not.

Herrod: That is a clear and simple way to state our difference, yes.

Socrates: Then how would you define murder?

Herrod: I? The onus of proof is on them, remember? They are the ones who introduced that terrible term. Why don't you cross-examine them?

Socrates: When I find one of them, I shall certainly do so. But for now, we are alone, you and I. What do *you* mean by *murder*?

Herrod: I suppose, killing an innocent human being.

Socrates: And do your opponents use the term in the same sense?

Herrod: They seem to call any killing murder.

Socrates: Do they call hunting animals for food murder?

Herrod: No, of course not.

Socrates: Why not?

Herrod: It's not killing human beings, of course.

Socrates: Do they call defensive warfare murder?

Herrod: No. They're usually hawks, not doves.

Socrates: What airy philosophers you have! And do they call it murder if the State executes a traitor or a murderer?

Defining murder: (1) killing (2) an innocent (3) human being

Herrod: No. They're not usually against capital punishment.

Socrates: Why not?

Herrod: I guess because it's not killing an *innocent* human being.

Socrates: Which was your definition of murder.

Herrod: Well... yes.

Socrates: So you agree on the definition of the term, at any rate.

Herrod: I suppose we do. But we do not agree that abortion should be called murder.

Socrates: Now then, let us see whether or not it fits your definition of murder. There are three parts to the definition. First, is abortion a case of killing?

(1) Is abortion killing?

Herrod: Terminating a pregnancy.

Socrates: Is the fetus killed?

Herrod: I do not like that emotional term.

Socrates: Your likes and dislikes are emotions, are they not?

Herrod: Of course.

Socrates: Then it is you who are treating the term emotionally rather than rationally.

Herrod: Only because they started it.

Socrates: You sound rather like a little child accused of fighting, saying: "He started it!" Perhaps so, but should you continue it? Is there not a better way? Should we not appeal to reason?

Herrod: Certainly.

Defining killing: (a) the object is a live organism

Socrates: Now, rationally, what does *killing* mean?

Herrod: I suppose it means forcibly putting a live organism to death.

Socrates: And is abortion's object a live organism?

Herrod: Of course.

Socrates: And is the term of the process its death?

(b) the term is death
(c) the means is forcible

Herrod: Yes.

Socrates: Is the death forcible?

Herrod: Yes.

Socrates: Then abortion is killing.

Herrod: Yes, but not murder.

Socrates: That is yet to be decided. Now to what definition of murder did we agree?

Herrod: Don't you remember?

Socrates: My memory sometimes plays tricks on me at my age.

Herrod: What *is* your age?

Socrates: You would not believe me if I told you.

Herrod: No, I suspect I wouldn't. And I also suspect that you are not really as forgetful as you pretend.

Socrates: It is of no consequence. But I trust *your* memory is in good health, at any rate. So please tell me: to what definition of murder did we agree?

Herrod: We agreed that murder is the killing of an innocent human being.

Socrates: Fine. Now let us see whether abortion comes under that definition, as they claim, or not, as you claim. First, we have agreed that abortion is killing, have we not?

Herrod: Yes.

Socrates: Second, is the fetus that is killed guilty of any crime or innocent?

(2) Is the fetus innocent?

Herrod: Not guilty, of course. But you can't call it innocent either unless it is a person. Cells aren't either guilty *or* innocent.

Socrates: But if it is a person, it would be innocent?

(3) Is the fetus a human being?

Herrod: If . . . yes.

Socrates: Then if the fetus is a human being, abortion will have to be called murder, for it fits all three parts of the definition.

If so, abortion is murder.

Herrod: Why all this shilly-shallying about words, Socrates? It's quite simple, really. Abortion is not murder because a fetus is *not* a person. Abortion is not killing a human being; it's helping a human being to terminate her unwanted pregnancy. That's all.

Socrates: You seem to be a bit impatient.

Herrod: Frankly, I *am* impatinet with all this word play. And I am also impatient with the direction in which you have turned the argument: focusing on the fetus rather than the mother.

Following the common master = following the argument wherever it leads

Socrates: I had hoped that it was not I but our common master that led us to that point.

Herrod: Our common master? What do you mean?

Socrates: Did we not agree to be rational? And being rational means following reason, following the argument wherever it leads, not following me or following you.

Herrod: The point we have been led to, whether by you or by reason, Socrates, is a very moot point: whether the fetus is a person. I would rather talk about less speculative matters, like the rights of women and social responsibilities and the legal aspects of the question.

Socrates: But what *you* would rather talk about should not lead us any more than what *I* would rather talk about. Unless we both agree to follow our common master, we will only follow each other, in a contest of wills, like two children playing King of the Mountain. Will you follow the common master or not?

Herrod: Oh, I want to be rational, all right. It's my opponents who are hysterical.

Socrates: Then you should not be reluctant to follow the argument.

Herrod: I'm not. But I am reluctant to be led from

clear, practical and answerable questions like the rights of women to murky, theoretical and unanswerable questions like whether a fetus is a person.

Socrates: If the question of the rights of women is so clear and answerable, why is there such disagreement about it?

Herrod: Well, the other question is not answerable, at any rate.

Socrates: How can you tell whether a question is answerable until you try to answer it?

Herrod: But it's so ... so damned theological!

Socrates: A strange word to use for the gods! But even if it were a theological question—which I do not see—why should it not still come under the rule of our common master?

Herrod: The common master settles rational questions. Theological questions are not rational questions. They are matters of faith, or superstition.

Socrates: Should we not investigate a thing before we classify it as superstitious? Wouldn't it be superstitious rather than rational to refuse to do so?

Herrod: But we can't investigate theology now.

Socrates: No, and I do not see why the question we *are* investigating now is theological at all. Why must we speak of the gods in order to speak of the fetus?

Herrod: I don't think we should. My opponents usually do.

Socrates: But they are not here now, are they? We are alone, we two.

Herrod: You said that before.

Socrates: Yes, and I shall say it again if the need arises.

Herrod: And you see the need arising?

Socrates: Yes, when you forget that it is *your* beliefs

How can you answer the question whether a fetus is a person?

How can you tell whether a question is answerable until you try to answer it?

Abortion not a theological question

and *your* actions that we are examining now.

Herrod: But it's *their* attack that I have to defend against.

Socrates: Yes, but in doing so we are not being led by your opponents, or by me, but by our common master, if only we will. Shall we continue to follow, or not?

Herrod: We shall.

Socrates: And that means following the argument wherever it leads. Will you do that? The argument is the common master's staff, as it were.

Herrod: I will follow the argument. Reason is my master. Faith is theirs.

Socrates: Who their master is, I do not know. They are not here. As to yourself—whether reason is your master or not is precisely what we are now investigating.

Herrod: Why do you call it the common master if not all follow it?

Socrates: Because it is like the light of the sun. It shines for all even though some shut their eyes or flee into the shadows. It is common like the light of day.

Herrod: Unlike faith.

The difference between faith and reason *Socrates:* Yes, unlike faith. Whether true or false, beliefs about the gods are neither plain nor common. They are mysteries, and they vary from place to place and from mind to mind. There are many different faiths, but not many different logics.

Herrod: I wholeheartedly agree with you, Socrates. I am skeptical of these obscurities too.

Socrates: I did not say I was skeptical of them, only that they were obscure, unlike reason. My question now is this: do you serve the common master and will you follow his argument?

Herrod: I said I would. Why do you continue to ask?

Socrates: You realize, do you not, that we have already come to the crucial point of the argument?

Herrod: You mean what the fetus is?

Socrates: Precisely.

Herrod: I don't think the abstract metaphysical status of the fetus *is* the crux of the argument.

Socrates: But if the fetus is a human person, it follows that abortion is murder, according to the argument.

Herrod: If, if, if! I think we're being led by the nose here. Abstract arguments can prove *anything.*

Socrates: Good arguments or bad ones?

Herrod: Bad ones, of course.

Socrates: And what is a bad argument? Is it not one which either uses its terms in an ambiguous way or begins with a false premise or fails to demonstrate that its conclusion necessarily follows from its premises?

Herrod: Right. Those are the three checkpoints of an argument. I took logic too, you know.

Socrates: Then let us look at the logic of the argument. First checkpoint: have we defined our terms wrongly? Have we used a term ambiguously?

Herrod: I don't think so. We were painstakingly careful.

Socrates: Let us skip the second checkpoint for a minute and ask about the third. Is the argument logically necessary? Does the conclusion follow? *If* one were to grant the premises, first, that killing an innocent human being is murder, and, second, that abortion is killing an innocent human being, does it not necessarily follow that abortion is murder?

Herrod: Yes, but...

Socrates: But you deny the premise.

Is the status of the fetus the crux of the argument?

Evaluating the argument: the three checkpoints

Herrod: That abortion is killing an innocent human being. Yes. The argument does not pass the second checkpoint.

Socrates: But abortion *is* killing, and the fetus *is* innocent—or not guilty, as you conceded.

Herrod: Yes, but not a human being.

The pro-abortionist must face the metaphysical question of the fetus.

Socrates: Ah, so you *are* facing up to the so-called abstract metaphysical question of the fetus.

Herrod: Harrumph.

Socrates: Why are you reluctant to do so?

Herrod: Because I'm a physician, not a metaphysician!

Socrates: I beg to differ with you, Doctor. Not everyone is a physician, but everyone is a metaphysician.

Herrod: What? Ridiculous. I know what I am.

Socrates: In that case you are a metaphysician. You know what you *are*.

Herrod: I think we need to define our terms.

Socrates: Those words are music to my ears!

Herrod: Somehow I thought you'd say something like that. All right, so what is metaphysics, O metaphysical musician?

Socrates: Simply thinking about being, thinking about what something *is*.

Herrod: And why must everyone think about being? I haven't seen much news about it in the papers lately.

Socrates: Suppose you were accused of murder because you ate a fish. How would you defend yourself?

Herrod: Are you joking or answering my question?

Socrates: I'm answering your question if you're answering mine. My answer is in your answer.

Herrod: But your question is silly, Socrates. No one would accuse me of murder for eating a fish.

Socrates: And why not?

Herrod: Why, because it isn't murder to eat a fish, of course.

Socrates: See? You're doing metaphysics. You're thinking about *is*-ness. Watch now; you'll do some more metaphysics.

Herrod: Not if I can help it.

Socrates: My point exactly: you can't. Now tell me, please: why is it not murder to eat a fish?

Herrod: Another silly question.

Socrates: And why *is* it murder to eat a human being? Why is cannibalism murder?

Herrod: Nothing but silly questions.

Socrates: If the fish you ate were human, would you not be a cannibal?

Herrod: Socrates, this is ridiculous.

Socrates: Why, pray tell?

Herrod: Why, because everyone knows a fish isn't human.

Socrates: You see? Everyone is a metaphysician.

Herrod: All right, so everyone is a metaphysician. So what?

Why everyone is a meta-physician

Socrates: To be a metaphysician—that is to know something of what *is*, is it not?

Herrod: Yes.

Socrates: Now—one more thing—when we know what is, does our knowing make what is? When we know that a fish is a fish and isn't a human, is it our knowledge that makes the fish a fish?

Does our knowledge change the nature of things known?

Herrod: Of course not. Unless science is only fantasy.

Socrates: Good! Now if someone were *not* to know what a fish is, would that change the fish itself?

Herrod: No . . . but it would change what the fish was *to him*. If I thought a fish were human, I would treat it differently.

Socrates: But if you did that—if you talked to it and brought it out of the water and put trousers on it— would it talk back to you and walk around?

Herrod: Of course not.

Socrates: So ignorance does not alter the nature of things any more than knowledge does.

Herrod: Of course not.

Socrates: Fine. Now let us consider the case of a slave. Is a slave a human being or not?

Herrod: A human being, of course.

Socrates: Does everyone know that?

Herrod: I don't think so. I think there were some people in the past who really thought slaves were of a subhuman species. In fact, didn't some people even in your enlightened Athens think that?

Socrates: To my shame, I admit it was so. But the ignorance of these people did not change the real nature of the slaves, did it?

Herrod: Of course not.

Socrates: And now let us talk about the fetus...

Is the nature of the fetus a matter of opinion?

Herrod: Oh, but that is a matter of opinion, Socrates, not a clear fact like a slave or a fish.

Socrates: Did we not agree that you are not a murderer if you ate a fish only because a fish *is* not a human being, whether anyone thinks so or not?

Herrod: Yes.

Socrates: And that you would be a murderer if you killed an innocent slave because a slave *is* a human being, whether anyone thinks so or not?

Herrod: Yes.

Socrates: So even though some think a fetus human and some do not, yet if it *is* human, one who kills it is a murderer. Does that not necessarily follow? Whether abortion is murder or not clearly depends on whether the fetus *is* a human being or not.

Herrod: No. It depends on whether we *call* it a human being or not. If we call it a person, abortion is murder. If we call it a group of cells, abortion is an operation.

Socrates: Whether we *call* abortion murder depends on whether we *call* the fetus a person. But whether abortion *is* murder depends on whether the fetus *is* a person, does it not?

Herrod: But it is a matter of opinion whether the fetus is a person or not. How dare you dogmatize about it!

Socrates: I did not say the fetus *is* a person, only that *if* it is, then abortion is murder.

Herrod: Well, no one knows that.

Socrates: Whether others know that or not, I do not know. Only you are here with me now. And what do you think we two should do when we do not know something, especially something as important as this?

Herrod: I suppose you want me to say, "We should seek the truth," or something like that.

Socrates: Something like that would be an excellent answer, yes.

Herrod: But the scientific facts are known to both sides, Socrates, and yet there remains this difference of opinion. It is a waste of time to argue about it; both sides have argued until they were blue in the face and neither side has been convinced or ever will be. The only policy in the face of such a difference of opinion is toleration, freedom of choice, pro-choice.

Socrates: So the question about the nature of the fetus cannot be answered? The difference of opinion cannot be resolved?

Herrod: No. I just said that.

If the fetus is human, then abortion is murder.

Can the question ever be resolved?

Socrates: How do you know that?

Herrod: I just told you that too. People have argued about it until they were blue in the face.

Socrates: And you? Have you argued about it until you were blue in the face?

Herrod: Of course not. Why waste time on a theoretical issue that never can be settled anyway?

How can you tell unless you try?

Socrates: Did we not agree a while back that the only way to tell whether a question is answerable or not is to try to answer it?

Herrod: Yes, and that is exactly what they have done, with no success.

Socrates: Until they were blue in the face.

Herrod: Yes.

Socrates: But they are not here now, are they? And you are not yet blue in the face.

Herrod: You keep saying that.

Socrates: You keep forgetting. You know, the word for *truth* in our language *(alētheia)* means literally "not-forgetting."

Herrod: That's true. I forgot.

Socrates: Touché. Now, back to the point. We admit, do we not, that the only way to tell whether a question is answerable or not is to try to answer it?

Herrod: Yes.

Socrates: And you see what follows with respect to the question about the fetus, do you not?

Herrod: Oh, all right. Go ahead. Try.

Socrates: Not without you. I am only your intellectual obstetrician, remember?

Herrod: Yes. But I assure you it will come to nothing. I hope you don't mind if I fortify myself with some more coffee before you begin.

Socrates: Before *we* begin. Go ahead. But I wonder at

your gift of foreknowledge. Are you a prophet?
Herrod: What do you mean?
Socrates: I marvel that you know a thing before it happens.
Herrod: What thing?
Socrates: That our attempt will come to nothing.
Herrod: That does not take a prophet to foretell, Socrates. Others have been down this road before.
Socrates: And they...
Herrod: ... are not here now, I know. I guess I'm just impatient.
Socrates: For what? For the truth or for something else?
Herrod: For the truth, of course, just like you. The common master, remember?
Socrates: I try to remember at all times. I serve the common master, too, but I hope I am not an impatient servant.
Herrod: How could it be wrong to be impatient for the truth?

Is it good to be impatient for truth?

Socrates: I think I can show you that. Would you say that for one who serves the common master the very first thing is to find the truth?
Herrod: Of course.
Socrates: That is how you are impatient. I would not agree with you there.
Herrod: What? I am astounded, Socrates, to hear that from *you*. What else comes before finding the truth?
Socrates: Might you consider *looking* for it first?
Herrod: (Silence. Tiny smile.)

What comes before finding the truth?

Socrates: That is the first time I have seen you smile, Doctor.
Herrod: (Longer silence. Larger smile.)
Socrates: Your second smile, Doctor. How eloquent

—more eloquent than my mere words, because it comes from the silence. I fear that far too many of my words come only from other words rather than from the silence. But now I am in the presence of wisdom— a gift from the gods, indeed, and a greater one than the gift of prophecy I jestingly ascribed to you before: the gift of silence and the learning of the first lesson— that we do not know. But it is I who am prattling on now and you who are wisely silent. Perhaps out of the silence can come a few words that are not prattle. We still have not investigated the question of the fetus, only talked about investigating it.

Herrod: Then let's begin.

Socrates: Profound words indeed, Doctor, truly attesting to your wisdom. Let the beginners begin. Now to find out whether a fetus is a person or not, I suppose we need to know what a person is. By the way, we have been using the terms *person* and *human beings* interchangeably. Which should we use, do you think?

Herrod: Human being. There may be intelligent beings on other planets that are not human, and we may want to call them persons too—Martian persons, for instance. Let's confine ourselves to earth.

What is a human being? *Socrates: Human being* it is, then—someone in this world. Well, now, what in the world *is* a human being?

Herrod: Oh, everyone knows what a human being is, Socrates. I need not tell you *that.*

Socrates: Oh dear; our wisdom seems to be leaving us. But perhaps a few questions can entice it to return. Please tell me this: when you say that *everyone* knows what a human being is, do you mean every cat and dog and tree and flower knows?

Herrod: Now you are being ridiculous again, Socrates. I wonder which of us has lost his wisdom now.

Socrates: I wonder that too. And I wonder whether you really wonder. But if not every cat and dog, every *what*? Please bear with my foolishness for a moment.

Herrod: Every human being, of course.

Socrates: *Every* human being knows what a human being is?

Herrod: Every normal human being, yes.

Socrates: And are you one of those normal human beings?

Herrod: Of course.

Socrates: Then please tell me, since you know. Do not, I pray, withhold this treasure of wisdom from my eager grasp.

Herrod: Socrates, this is silly. A human being is what you see before you. People like us. Like me, anyway; I'm not too sure about you.

Socrates: But I did not ask for *examples* of human beings, which are many, but for the common nature of all human beings, which is one. A definition tells the common nature of a species, does it not? So please tell me what this is; what makes all of us humans human?

Herrod: In other words, define a person.

Socrates: Yes, if you now want to use the terms interchangeably.

Herrod: Well... we are conscious.

Socrates: Are animals conscious too?

Herrod: In a sense.

Socrates: I think you know what my next question will be.

Herrod: I can guess.

Socrates: Guess then.

Herrod: Suppose I do guess your questions. Suppose I play the part of the questioner for a while, and you answer.

Socrates: If you think we may progress toward our goal better in this way, let us try it, by all means. Ask away, and I shall answer as best I can with my tiny hoard of wisdom.

Human vs. animal consciousness

Herrod: Let's begin with this question: in what sense is a cat or a dog conscious?

Socrates: Do you want me to tell the truth or to hazard a wild guess?

Herrod: To tell the truth, of course.

Socrates: Well, then, to tell the truth, I don't know how a cat or a dog is conscious because I am not a cat or a dog, nor have I ever found one who would answer questions about itself.

Herrod: I thought you were going to cooperate.

Socrates: I'm perfectly willing to cooperate if only you ask me a question I can answer. Ask me about human beings, and I shall give you an answer from my own experience. But I have no cat experience or dog experience from which to give you an answer.

Herrod: You have observed cats and dogs, have you not?

Socrates: Many times.

Herrod: Then you have some experience of animal behavior.

Socrates: Yes.

Behavior exhibits consciousness

Herrod: And doesn't behavior exhibit consciousness? Don't we judge of a sleeping person that he is unconscious because we observe a certain pattern of behavior—eyes closed, body still, breathing slow and steady? And don't we judge of a waking person that he is wakingly conscious because we observe a different behavior?

Socrates: Both your science and your logic are impeccable, Doctor. It is as you say.

Herrod: Then you do know something of animal consciousness, since you observe animal behavior, and behavior exhibits consciousness.

Socrates: Wisdom seems to be returning to us. Our experiment of reversing our roles seems to be working.

Herrod: Then answer my next question: what is the difference between human consciousness and animal consciousness, as exhibited by behavior? You need not tell me what animals have that we lack, only the reverse: what do we have that animals lack? That is a question that has puzzled many scientists and philosophers and continues to do so. If you can give a simple and true answer to that question, you must be wiser than all those puzzled people who can't.

Socrates: Now I am among the puzzled, too, because I know I am not wiser than all those others, and yet I do know a very simple answer to your question. And we have known it for a very long time, we humans.

Herrod: Well? Don't keep me in suspense. What is it?

Socrates: There has been no suspense for 2400 years, since we philosophers defined man as a rational animal. Surely this has been reported by now? It's hardly news.

*Man as
rational
animal*

Herrod: But Socrates, if you are content with that old saw, distinguishing us from the animals by having reason, you will run into a mare's nest of problems. For one thing, this is not an "operational definition," as we say: it doesn't specify any observable behavior. But you admitted that consciousness was exhibited by behavior. What behavior is specifically rational? Second, how can you distinguish human reasoning from computer reasoning, artificial intelligence? You do know about computers, don't you?

Socrates: Yes, I have read your entire library. And it seems even simpler to distinguish us from computers than from animals, and to do so "operationally," as you say.

Herrod: I would like to hear this "simple" thing from you. And please do not answer that we are different from animals in having reason and different from computers in having feelings, because then we would be just animals plus computers. Please tell me the one thing that distinguishes us from both. What do we have that neither animals nor computers have? And remember, it must be exhibited in behavior.

Socrates: What an easy question to answer! There is something that human reason does that no computer or animal ever does.

Herrod: Well? What is it?

Socrates: You mean you really don't know?

Herrod: No, and neither does the rest of the academic world, which is full of learned professors in beards and spectacles running around with clipboards, who claim that their computers think.

Socrates: But these professors are not here now, are they?

Herrod: No, but I am. And I want to know.

Socrates: But you have just answered your own question.

Herrod: What? What do you mean?

Socrates: You really don't know?

Herrod: No, I really don't know. Tell me!

Socrates: Again you have just answered your own

How are humans distinct from animals plus computers?

The question is its own answer.

question.

Herrod: Stop playing games with me. This is a serious question.

Socrates: And you want to know the answer.

Herrod: Yes.

Socrates: That is your answer: the will to know. No computer and no animal is a philosopher, a lover and pursuer of wisdom. In plain and simple terms of observable behavior, no computer or animal does what we have been doing: asking questions. Even if computers reason—which I do not grant—they do not *will* to. The one thing you never observe a computer do is to question its programming—unless it is programmed to do so, and then it does not question *that* programming. Unless it is programmed to do so. There is always an unquestioned program; everything is done in obedience to that. Computers are obedient; reason is disobedient. We are obedient to reason by being disobedient to our programming, by questioning our programming. We have been told by our parents or teachers to think certain things, but we question them. We are philosophers.

No animal or computer questions

Herrod: I am a doctor.

Socrates: You are a human being; therefore you are a philosopher. You want to know. You just told me that three times.

Herrod: Your simplicity astounds me, Socrates. But I cannot refute it.

Socrates: Why do you wish to refute it?

Herrod: I am suspicious of simple answers.

Socrates: Why? Because you think they are probably not true, or for some other reason?

Herrod: Not true, of course.

Socrates: Then you desire the truth?

Herrod: Of course.

Socrates: Then you too are simple-minded, like myself.

*Back to
the main
argument* *Herrod:* Hmmmph! Not so simple-minded, I think, that I can find my way back to the main road of our argument. We turned off the road to talk about animals and computers and reason; where do we get back on?

Socrates: We needed a definition of a human being, remember?

Herrod: Ah, yes.

Socrates: And we have one—a very old one, in fact. Man is a rational animal, one who wills to know.

Herrod: Where do we go from here?

Socrates: Wherever the argument leads us. Let us recall why we needed a definition of a human being.

Herrod: Oh, yes. To find out whether the fetus was a human being. Aha! Here we are. Do we ever observe a fetus asking questions?

Socrates: No.

Herrod: And a human being is one who questions?

Socrates: Yes.

*Apparently,
a fetus
is not a
human
being
because it
is not
rational.* *Herrod:* Ergo, a fetus is not a human being, and therefore abortion is not murder. *Quod erat demonstrandum. Finis. Consummatum est.* Case closed.

Socrates: Ah... do you mind if I return to my role as questioner for just a minute or two? There might be one or two loose ends, so to speak, that we would want to tie up in packaging our argument—a few things we may have forgotten, perhaps. If not, we will be doubly sure our argument is complete by this tedious review. So please bear with me for just a tiny bit more. One thing still bothers me.

Herrod: What's that? The argument seems pretty cut-

and-dried to me. Must you question *everything* I say?

Socrates: I want to question something *I* said. I wonder whether I was right in defining a human being as one who asks questions.

Herrod: Why do you wonder that now?

Socrates: Consider an infant. Would you call it a human being?

*Is an
infant
a human
being?*

Herrod: Of course. Oh, I see. You are asking for the difference between abortion and infanticide. Well, now . . .

Socrates: No, I am asking whether you would call an infant a human being. One question at a time, if you please.

Herrod: Yes, an infant is a human being.

Socrates: And does an infant ask questions?

Herrod: No.

Socrates: Then perhaps we should not have defined a human being as one who asks questions. And here is another case: is there not a state called dreamless sleep? Do you ever sleep at night without dreaming?

Herrod: Not only at night but also sometimes during the day; for instance, when someone bores me with abstract arguments.

Socrates: I praise your will to pursue the truth even though your feelings are bored. Now then, when you sleep without dreams, do you ask questions?

Herrod: I don't think so.

Socrates: And if I should kill you in your sleep, would I be guilty of murder?

Herrod: Of course you would. I don't stop being a person when I fall asleep; I stop *functioning* rationally when I sleep.

Socrates: So there is a difference between *being* a person and *functioning* as a person? (We seem to have

*The
distinction
between
being a
person and
functioning
as a
person*

drifted into the habit of using the terms *person* and *human being* interchangeably, despite our earlier decision not to do so.)

Herrod: Yes. Being a person is not necessarily functioning as one.

Socrates: So that an infant and a sleeper, who cannot function as persons, nevertheless are persons?

Herrod: Yes.

Socrates: Then the fact that the fetus does not yet function as a person does not prove it *is* not a person.

Herrod: No, but it doesn't prove that it *is,* either.

Socrates: What is it, then? Is it a fish?

Is the fetus only a potential person?

Herrod: It is a *potential* human being. If we say the fetus is a person only because it will grow into one, we confuse the actual with the potential.

Socrates: A useful distinction, Doctor; one of the great conceptual tools of my intellectual grandson, Aristotle. But a potential X must be an actual Y. If the fetus is not an actual person, what *is* it actually?

Herrod: I don't know.

Socrates: And yet you kill it?

Is abortion murder because it kills potential persons?

Herrod: Wait a minute! Are you saying a fetus is a person just because it is a potential person?

Socrates: No.

Herrod: I should hope not, because if so, then a single spermatazoon or a single ovum is also a person, and spermicide becomes homicide. In fact, even the primordial slime that evolved into us during ten million years or so is a potential person, and slime-killing becomes murder.

Socrates: Ah, yes. Our Father Slime. I found it a fascinating experience to read your science library and meet your new gods. A real advance upon ours. We thought ourselves to be bastards of the gods above, in our foolishness, rather than legitimate children of the slime below. We knew so very little about the true gods, it seems.

Herrod: What *did* you know about?

Socrates: Oh, only simple, childish things you have outgrown—things like birth and death and reason and virtue.

Herrod: Do I detect a note of sarcasm, Socrates? Are you maligning modern science?

Socrates: Certainly not. Would I malign my own great-grandchild? Your modern *philosophies*, now, that's quite another thing.

Herrod: Then you would have no objection to talking science rather than philosophy?

Socrates: Indeed not. And now let us return to our question and talk science about it. What is the fetus?

Herrod: Oh. I thought we were talking about the primordial slime.

Socrates: Is your work here to abort slime?

Herrod: No.

Socrates: Then let us return to our question: what is a fetus?

Herrod: Socrates, your single-minded concern about the fetus bothers me.

Socrates: That is an interesting fact about your psyche, but it does not alter the argument.

Herrod: You are looking at the thing only from the fetus's point of view. You are ignoring the mother. I suppose you will soon be calling abortion "killing a baby" instead of "terminating a pregnancy."

Socrates: If that is what it *is*, yes. I am led only by what a thing is. And how else *is* the pregnancy terminated except by killing the baby, or the fetus, if you prefer?

Herrod: But you are ignoring the mother.

Socrates: I certainly do not want to do that, because the mother *is*. Perhaps we can turn to her after we finish investigating the fetus.

Herrod: The fetus, the fetus, always this concern for the fetus. You're a fetus fetishist—a fetus-ist.

Two reasons for concern for the fetus

Socrates: I have at least two reasons for wanting to know what the fetus is. You have just reminded me of one of them in reminding me that I ought to think about the mother too.

Herrod: What's that?

(1) It is

Socrates: Just as the mother *is*, and I ought to think about her because she *is*, so the fetus also *is*, and I ought to think about it for the very same reason. Would it be honest of either of us to ignore what *is*?

Herrod: Well... no.

(2) It is the victim

Socrates: And my second reason is that the fetus is the victim.

Herrod: Must you use such language?

Socrates: If it is appropriate to what *is*, yes. Let us look and try to find out whether it is appropriate or not. What would you say a victim is? Is it not one who is harmed?

Herrod: Yes.

Socrates: And is not the fetus harmed by killing it?

Herrod: The mother is serviced.

Socrates: Is the fetus "serviced"?

Herrod: Fetus, fetus! You keep turning from the mother to the fetus.

Socrates: No, Doctor, *you* keep turning away from the fetus to the mother. We were discussing the fetus, if you remember.

Herrod: Socrates, look at it this way. Here is why it is reasonable to consider the mother rather than the fetus. Suppose I were in the business of fumigating trees with a powerful pesticide. I would be servicing the trees by eliminating the unwanted life form, the fungus. Wouldn't it be silly to think only of the fungus and not of the trees, or to think as much about the fungus as about the trees? Our primary concern should be with the more valuable life form—in the one case, the trees, in the other case, the mother.

Is the fetus a lesser life form?

Socrates: But you beg the question with your analogy. The analogy will work only if the fetus is to the mother what the fungus is to the trees: a less valuable life form, a pest to be eliminated. But is that not precisely what is in question here: whether the fetus is a human person, like the mother, or a lesser life form? We must go back to that question: what is the fetus? Will you continue to follow the argument, as you promised? and in scientific terms, as you preferred?

Herrod: I suppose I must.

Socrates: Good. I learned from your science library that each person has a single, unique genetic code, just as everyone has a unique set of fingerprints. Is that correct?

The scientific argument: the genetic code

Herrod: Oh, Socrates, that argument won't work.

Socrates: What argument? I am only gathering data, not arguing yet.

Herrod: All right. One thing at a time.

Socrates: Precisely. Now in that genetic code is every bodily feature in potentiality, is it not? a program ready for the computer, so to speak? everything from eye color and brain size to a tendency to warts?

Herrod: Correct.

Socrates: And every person has his or her unique genetic code in every cell of the body, correct?

Herrod: Yes.

Socrates: This complete genetic code for a person—is it found in the primordial slime?

Herrod: Of course not.

Socrates: In a fish?

Herrod: No.

Socrates: An ape?

Herrod: No.

Socrates: You see what we are doing: approaching the fetus. But before we arrive, let us approach from the opposite direction, so to speak. Is this genetic code complete in me now?

Herrod: Yes.

Socrates: Is it in me when I sleep?

Herrod: Yes.

Socrates: Was it in me when I was one year old?

Herrod: Yes.

Socrates: One minute old?

Herrod: Yes.

Socrates: One minute before I was born?

Genetically, we begin at conception.

Herrod: Yes. It is present from conception.

Socrates: So the fetus has it all during the time between conception and birth?

Herrod: Yes, but that does not prove what you want it to prove, Socrates, that a fetus is a person.

Socrates: I want only to follow the argument wherever it leads. I thought we agreed about that.

Herrod: We did. But the argument has not proved that the fetus is a person.

Socrates: Nor did I say that it did. One step at a time, please. Now the sperm a moment before conception does not have the complete genetic code, isn't that so? It has only half the code and half the chromosomes?

Herrod: Yes. It is haploid, not diploid.

Socrates: And the same is true of the egg?

Herrod: Yes. We should say *spermatozoa* and *ovum*, to be exact.

Socrates: And the fertilized egg does have the full set of chromosomes and the complete genetic code?

Herrod: The zygote—yes, it has the complete genetic code.

Socrates: And is that code the mother's?

Herrod: Of course not. Each one is different.

Socrates: Each *what* is different?

Herrod: Each code.

Socrates: But the code is the code *of* or *for* something, is it not?

Herrod: Yes.

Socrates: What is that something?

Herrod: The fetus, of course. But you have not proved it is a person.

Socrates: I am a person, am I not?

Herrod: Of course.

Socrates: And I have my own unique genetic code, do I not?

Herrod: Yes.

Socrates: Is it the same code as that of the fetus in my mother's womb that grew into what I am now?

Herrod: Yes.

Socrates: And am I still a fetus?

Herrod: Of course not.

Socrates: Then we cannot use the word *fetus* in place of the word *something* when we say that the genetic code is the code of *something*. I have the code, and I am not a fetus, therefore not everything that has the code is a fetus.

Herrod: I'm getting impatient with this abstract word play.

Of what is the genetic code the code?

Socrates: Does a good scientist get impatient with his data?

Herrod: No.

Socrates: But words are the philosopher's data, or hold the data, so to speak, as houses hold people. We do not *play* with our word-data; we gather and question it, as you scientists gather and question your empirical data. We take words seriously as you take instrument readings seriously. Now what word shall we put in place of the word *fetus* when we say the genetic code is the code *of* something?

Herrod: Organism. A fetus is an organism that is a potential person; we are organisms that are actual persons.

*Why is
the fetus
not an
actual
person?* *Socrates:* And now we need only one more answer from you to complete your defense. Why is the fetus only a potential person and not an actual person?

Herrod: Because a person is an individual, and a fetus is not yet an individual.

Socrates: Your syllogism is logical, but we must now prove the premise that the fetus is not an individual. We have just admitted that it *is* an individual genetically, have we not?

Herrod: Well then, let's not define a person genetically.

Socrates: Well, well. It seems our scientific definition of a person is to be abandoned rather quickly. To what do we turn instead?

Herrod: To common sense. What do ordinary people think of when they think of a person? Not genetics.

Socrates: What, then?

*The fetus
is part
of the
mother.* *Herrod:* Look here: the fetus is only a part of the mother: a single cell at first, then many cells, part of her body. It is not an individual because it is part of

another individual. Ah, there we have the argument: another syllogism to prove the premise of the first one. A fetus is part of another individual (the mother); and no individual person is part of another individual person; therefore the fetus is not an individual person. It is individual existence that counts.

Socrates: Aha! Metaphysics.

Herrod: All right, metaphysics. But persons are not parts of other persons, and the fetus is a part of the mother. Therefore the fetus is not a person. Now there's a solid metaphysical argument for you!

How can a person be part of another person?

Socrates: It certainly seems solid—as solid as this cement block here in the wall. May I examine your argument by asking a question about this cement block?

Herrod: What?

Socrates: I said...

Herrod: I heard what you said. I just didn't believe it.

Socrates: But do you believe this is a cement block?

Herrod: Yes, but...

Socrates: And is this block a part of this wall?

Herrod: Yes. What is the point of this nonsense?

Socrates: Patience, my good doctor. A good doctor has a lot of patience. Bear with me, please. Now this wall here—is it part of the hospital building?

Herrod: Yes.

Socrates: Now does it follow from the two things we have said that the cement block is part of the building? Since it is part of the wall and the wall is part of the building?

Herrod: Yes.

Socrates: One more example, if you please. Your toe is part of your foot, is it not?

Herrod: Must you tediously multiply examples?

Socrates: I want to be sure of the principle involved. I must explore the case of the toe as well as the case of the cement block to be sure the principle works for living things as well as nonliving.

Herrod: All right, my toe is part of my foot.

Socrates: And your foot is part of your body?

Herrod: Yes.

Socrates: And therefore your toe is part of your body?

Herrod: Yes.

Socrates: Do you see the principle we have uncovered in all this talk about parts?

Herrod: I think so. If A is part of B and B is part of C, then A must be part of C.

Socrates: Excellent. You have a sharp mind, Doctor Herrod.

Herrod: I also have a good education. In logic that is called a transitive relation.

Socrates: Yes. Now please answer for one more case: how many feet does a fetus have, once the feet develop?

Herrod: If it develops normally, two, of course.

Socrates: And how many feet does the mother have?

Herrod: Two, of course.

Socrates: Not four?

Herrod: What? Now you're being ridiculous again, Socrates. Why would you say that?

*Reductio
ad absurdum:
does a
pregnant
woman
have four
feet?*

Socrates: The feet of the fetus are part of the fetus, are they not?

Herrod: Yes.

Socrates: And the fetus is a part of the mother, you say?

Herrod: Yes.

Socrates: Then since the relation of part to whole is transitive, the parts of the fetus are parts of the mother.

Herrod: Oh. I guess we made a mistake somewhere.

Socrates: I should think so. Think what absurdities we would get ourselves into if we continued along this line of thought. If the fetus is male, it would force us to say that his mother had a penis.

Herrod: Obviously we went off the track somewhere.

Socrates: I think so. Let us review the argument that brought us here to find out where we were derailed. Were we wrong to agree to the principle that if A is part of B and B part of C, then A must be part of C?

Herrod: No, that was not wrong.

Socrates: And were we wrong when we said that the feet or the penis were parts of the fetus?

Herrod: No.

Socrates: Then there is only one other place where we could have gone off the tracks. The only other premise was that the fetus is a part of the mother.

Herrod: But if we deny that, what is to stop our opponents' train from chugging straight down the track?

Socrates: Nothing but irrationality, Doctor. The argument seems to be a juggernaut.

Herrod: Wait a minute. Let's back up and reconsider our premises.

Socrates: A few minutes ago it was *I* who wanted to back up and you who were announcing *finis*!

Herrod: I was too hasty. I thought I knew what I did not know.

Socrates: I am awestruck. You have been visited by the oracle.

Herrod: Or by one who himself has been visited by the oracle. Your learned ignorance seems to be a communicable disease.

Socrates: So now you know who I really am.

Herrod: You play your part well, at any rate.

False premise: the fetus is part of the mother.

Socrates: It is never difficult to play the part of one-self.

Herrod: I do not believe in reincarnation.

Socrates: Actually, neither do I. When I suggested it to Plato, he took me much too seriously. It was meant only as a "likely story," like the stories of the gods.

Herrod: Where have you come from, then?

Socrates: I'm afraid I could not explain it to you very well. Reincarnation is not a *wholly* bad guess. But the truth about where I come from is so much more, and so astonishing, and so difficult to put into words without stretching them beyond the limits of your understanding, that I despair of answering your question. Please just accept me as I am and let us get on with two much more important matters: my work here and yours.

Herrod: But I just can't help wondering who you really are. When you referred to the oracle before, you meant the oracle of Apollo at Delphi, didn't you? You weren't quoting but remembering!

Socrates: Remembering?

Herrod: Remembering the famous incident when the oracle told you that you were the wisest man in the world because you knew that you knew nothing.

Socrates: Yes, but you have the story wrong in three ways. First, it was my friend Chaerephon, not myself, who visited and heard the oracle. Second, the message was not that I was wiser than anyone else, only that no one was wiser than I. Third, the reason for my wisdom was not specified by the oracle. I deduced the reason: it was not that I knew that I had no *knowledge*, but that I knew that I had no *wisdom*: a much more rare and godlike thing. In fact, only the gods

*Socrates
and the
Delphic
oracle*

have it; we *pursue* it. Thus we become philosophers: lovers and friends of wisdom.

Herrod: You play your part very well indeed.

Socrates: So do you.

Herrod: What? I am not playing a part. I really am Doctor Herrod.

Socrates: You really are Herrod, but *are* you Doctor?

Herrod: What do you mean?

Socrates: Being a doctor—is that not your function, your profession?

Herrod: Yes.

Socrates: And did we not agree a while ago that there was a distinction between being something and functioning as something?

Herrod: Yes.

Socrates: You would still be Herrod if you functioned as a lawyer, would you not? In fact, you are still Herrod when you are asleep and not functioning in any specifically human way at all—almost like the fetus, shall we say?

Herrod: Oh, *that.*

Socrates: Yes, that. We are not here to bandy words about ourselves or each other, but to examine those words to try to find the truth about what you do. *Back to the argument*

Herrod: We've been at it for an hour now, and we've failed. I want to go home.

Socrates: Why do you say we have failed? *Has the argument failed?*

Herrod: We have been fishing in the ocean of words with the fishing line of logic and we have come up empty.

Socrates: I seem to recall a rather different result of our fishing expedition: we found a fish at the end of our line, but it was not the fish we wanted. So we tried to throw it back. But it is still with us. It seems *It has landed the wrong fish.*

to be a shark, that threatens to devour us.

Herrod: What can we do?

Socrates: If we serve the common master, we must do *something* with our shark. We cannot simply pretend he isn't there. We must either throw him back or be eaten alive.

Herrod: Are those the only two possibilities?

Socrates: If we are rational, yes. Either we answer the objection or concede the point.

Herrod: You serve a severe master.

Socrates: And you?

Herrod: (Sigh.)

Socrates: Why do you hesitate?

Herrod: It seems I must choose—not just about this argument and not just about abortion, but about the common master first.

Socrates: Yes, you are wise to perceive that order of priorities and also the fact that the common master must be freely chosen. He will not force himself upon us. He is like the light: gentle. If we choose to close our eyelids, he will not shine through them against our will.

Herrod: I can do no less than you if I am honest. Let us continue to follow this severe master.

Socrates: Splendid! Your faith bodes well for our reasoning.

Herrod: Faith? I have no faith.

Socrates: Oh, but you do, if you choose to serve the master. But let that pass for now. How do you intend to throw back the fish that you have caught?

Herrod: Suppose we backtrack.

Socrates: Usually that is the surest way to progress.

Herrod: Let's look this shark full in the face. It is as if he had two rows of teeth; together they devour me and my work. The two rows of teeth are the two premises of the argument. The first premise is that killing an innocent human being is murder, and the second is that abortion is killing an innocent human being, that the fetus is a person. The conclusion follows only from both premises together. Now if we could pull either row of teeth, we would not be devoured. The teeth of the remaining premise would have nothing to chew against.

The two premises of the argument are like a shark's two rows of teeth.

Socrates: An apt image indeed, and a clear analysis of the argument. The doctor seems to have become a dentist. Which row of teeth do you hope to remove? Not any wisdom teeth, I hope.

Herrod: Let's try the two rows one by one. First, the first premise. Must we admit that all killing of innocent human beings is murder?

(1) Is killing an innocent person always murder?

Socrates: Can you think of any exception to the principle?

Herrod: Let me think a minute . . .

Socrates: An excellent idea!

Herrod: Don't be sarcastic.

Socrates: I wasn't.

Herrod: Here—what about the unintended killing of civilians in a bombing raid that is necessary to destroy an evil enemy's military installations? Unintended killing is not murder. Oh, but I see that will not help us. Obviously, abortion does not kill the fetus unintentionally.

Socrates: You seem to be following the common master well.

Herrod: Why? Because I seem to be coming over to your position?

Socrates: No, because you are being rational. Must I remind you again? I serve only the common master, not any one position. I begin only with doubt and hope to end in some certainties. You began in certainties and have now progressed to doubts. Both can be ways of serving the common master.

Herrod: Somehow I do not feel comfortable in that service.

Socrates: I never promised you comfort.

Herrod: Afflict the comfortable and comfort the afflicted, eh?

Socrates: A wise saying. For if we begin with the first, we may hope for the second. The affliction of the mind is the only road I know to the comfort of knowing.

(2) Can we deny the humanity of the fetus?

Herrod: I suppose we must return to my affliction, the argument. It seems we must try to pull the other row of teeth in my shark, the second premise. If we could maintain that the person begins at some time later than conception, we could justify at least some abortions. Let's see now ... oh, of course! Here's the argument—how simple! Look here: you date your existence from birth, not from conception. Everyone does. You are fifty years old on your fiftieth birthday, not fifty and three-quarters years old, which is what you would be if you dated your existence from conception.

We date existence from birth, not conception.

Socrates: Actually, I believe some people do date from conception. Didn't the Chinese do that?

Herrod: Perhaps that is the exception that proves the rule.

Socrates: I cannot understand that saying; how can an exception *prove* a rule? An exception *disproves* a general rule.

But dating is only a convention.

Herrod: Why must you question every cliché? Never mind. Anyway, it is only a social custom, an artifice.

The Chinese didn't *make* the fetus human by dating it from conception.

Socrates: Indeed not. And other peoples, who choose the other artifice, equally do not make the fetus non-human by dating it from birth, do they?

Herrod: Well, no. But it all seems to be relative.

Socrates: What *all* seems to be relative to *what*? This *it* and this *all* of yours seem to be relative, all right: relative to whatever you want to insert into these vague categories. Surely you don't mean that everything, without exception, is relative?

Is it all relative?

Herrod: How do you know what I mean? Quite possibly I mean just that.

Socrates: I don't think so. I think you know too much logic and too much science to make such a silly mistake.

Herrod: What logic? What science?

Socrates: Too much logic because you know that a self-contradiction cannot be true, and your idea of absolute relativism is just that: a self-contradiction. And too much science because you know there *are* things that are not relative—to our opinion, at any rate, though they may be relative to each other: things like birds and stones and atoms and gravity and mass and number.

Herrod: Ah, but those are hard facts. Dating the beginning of human personhood is not a hard fact but a matter of opinion.

Socrates: *Dating* is surely not a hard fact, because it depends on us. But what is dated is a different matter, is it not? Whether you say you are fifty years old since birth or fifty and three-quarters since conception is an artifice. But the hard fact is that you were born fifty years ago and conceived fifty and three-quarters years ago. There must be something real for our measures to measure, mustn't there?

Herrod: Of course. But humanness is not one of those hard facts that can be measured.

Socrates: It seems not, at least to you. Let us explore this "seems" to see whether it proves to be an "is," as you claim. Are you with me still in the discipleship of the argument?

Herrod: I suppose I am.

Socrates: You do not sound like an enthusiastic disciple.

Herrod: I'm getting tired. I need another cup of coffee.

Socrates: How wonderfully you people trust your coffee to ferry you over troubled waters!

Herrod: Don't you want any?

Socrates: No, I love to plunge into the waters.

Herrod: So I've noticed.

Socrates: Let us get on with our investigation. What hard facts do we have to help us decide what the fetus is?

Herrod: I think we both know the facts. We just interpret them differently. And that's a matter of opinion, which can't be settled by the facts themselves.

Socrates: Is a good interpretation faithful to the facts?

Herrod: Yes.

Socrates: And a bad interpretation is not?

Herrod: Yes.

Socrates: Then let us test these two interpretations by the facts themselves.

Herrod: All right. Look at the differences between the zygote and the adult person. Those who call abortion murder say that a person begins at conception, that the zygote is a person. So they must say there is a greater difference between prezygote and zygote than between zygote and adult, since the first difference, they say, is a difference in kind, between nonperson and person, while the second is only a difference in degree, between two stages of growth of a person. It is this claim, I feel sure, we will be able to see as absurd. Surely you see the enormous difference between a zygote and yourself: a far greater difference than that between prezygote and zygote.

Socrates: I see nothing until I look. Let me look now. I see a great difference in size with my imagination. But the question is whether I can see a difference in kind with my reason.

Herrod: How can you determine such an abstract thing?

Socrates: Let us begin with something we do know. What are the differences between an infant and an adult?

Herrod: Why waste time with that question? I asked about the differences between zygote and adult.

Socrates: Patience, please, Doctor. We will get to that.

Herrod: But everybody knows the differences between an infant and an adult. Why is it necessary to go into this if we all know it?

Socrates: Is it possible to forget what we know?

Herrod: Yes.

Socrates: Then let us take some care that we do not forget this thing that we know. Let us take the minor risk, that of wasting a few minutes of time, to avoid the major risk, that of forgetting a simple and important fact.

Herrod: You are really very tedious, you know.

Socrates: I'm sorry. It's just my way, my only way of thinking. Quicker minds than mine can leap into the

What are the differences between infant and adult?

truth like Tarzan leaping from a vine. (Yes, I read your Tarzan stories too.) But my mind can only crawl like an inchworm, inch by laborious inch, making sure every step of the way.

Herrod: But once you know something, however slowly you find it, you then know it.

Socrates: Alas, perhaps my mind is more fickle and frivolous than any other mind on earth, but I seem to be terribly forgetful. I find that even very evident truths are easily forgotten if I do not put forth the effort to keep them in mind. My mind seems to be like a large birdcage, and any of the birds seem ready to fly away if only I relax my watch.

Herrod: You are a very strange person, Socrates.

Socrates: Then would you please tell this very strange person what these differences are that everyone knows between an infant and an adult?

The differences:

(1) size *Herrod:* All right. Let's see . . . for one thing, infants are obviously much smaller.

Socrates: That's one. What else?

(2) development *Herrod:* They are much less developed in all their bodily systems.

Socrates: That's two. Anything else?

(3) dependence *Herrod:* They are more dependent on their mother for survival.

Socrates: Three. Any others?

(4) mobility *Herrod:* Hmm . . . that seems to include just about everything, unless we want to make mobility a separate difference. The infant does not move much unless moved, while the adult roams about at will.

Socrates: Fine. That's four. Is that all?

Herrod: It seems to be, yes.

Socrates: Now—one more question before we return to the fetus, if you will only be so good as to extend your patience just one more minute. Do any of these four differences we have just mentioned make a difference as to whether killing is murder or not? For instance, can we say that it is murder to kill a large person but not a small person? Or is it worse to kill a larger person?

Are these differences morally relevant?

Is it worse to kill an adult than a child?

Herrod: I don't want to say that. But I do want to say that the degree of development might count.

Socrates: Would you say that it is not murder, or less serious murder, to kill a preadolescent child, whose reproductive system is not fully developed, than to kill a late adolescent, whose system is complete?

Herrod: Of course not. But it does seem to me worse to kill an adult than a ten-minute-old infant. The degree of development does seem morally relevant.

Socrates: Let us see if this "seems" is an "is." If the degree of development makes a moral difference, then a great difference in degree of development would make a great moral difference, and a small difference in development would make a small difference in morality. Does that follow logically?

Herrod: Yes.

Socrates: Then if it is much worse to kill an adult than an infant, it would be a little worse to kill a late adolescent than a preadolescent.

Herrod: That certainly seems wrong.

Socrates: And it would also be not such a terrible thing to molest or beat or kill small children as large ones.

Herrod: No, no. If anything, it's worse. The small ones are less able to defend themselves. Everyone detests child molesting. We went off the track somewhere with these strange consequences.

Socrates: With our principle, I think. The absurd

consequences necessarily follow from your false principle.

Herrod: What false principle?

Socrates: That the victim's size or degree of development makes a difference to the morality of killing. Do you retract that principle now?

Herrod: I suppose I must.

Socrates: You hesitate. You are not sure of this?

Herrod: I just think I see where the admission will take me.

Socrates: One thing at a time, please. We are rowing a boat downstream, and you are looking around the next bend of the river instead of making sure of the stroke of the oar right now.

Herrod: That's because I foresee where the current is taking my boat.

Socrates: And you would like to beach your boat and abandon the stream entirely.

Herrod: Yes.

Socrates: But the stream is the argument.

Herrod: Yes.

Socrates: And we agreed to follow the argument wherever it takes us, did we not?

Herrod: Yes.

Socrates: And the argument has led us to this question: is any one of the four differences we found between infant and adult morally relevant? Is it, for instance, less evil to kill a dependent or immobile victim

than an independent or mobile one? a paralytic, for example?

Herrod: Of course not. And I know where the argument will take us next, Socrates. You will say that the fetus differs from an infant only by these four things: it is smaller, less developed, more dependent, and less mobile. And since none of these factors is morally relevant, it follows that it is just as much murder to kill a fetus as to kill an infant.

Socrates: That is a very strong and simple way of putting the argument.

Herrod: Your argument, Socrates. I just anticipated you. All this talk about *the* argument—maybe that's just a smoke screen. I feel manipulated.

Socrates: May I point out that the latest and strongest argument was yours, not mine?

Herrod: It wasn't my argument, Socrates. I just formulated it.

Socrates: I couldn't have put it better myself. "My" arguments too are not mine; I am only their formulator. It is the river, not my oar, that carries our boat. My oar only steers the boat away from the rocks of self-contradiction; it is the stream that gives the direction. Or to use still another image, the arguments are like paths through a forest: we explore them, or we map them, but we do not make them. The roads the mind walks are just as objective as the roads the body walks, you know, and lead to mental places just as different as the different physical places.

Herrod: I don't think I buy that simple-minded notion of objective truth, Socrates. But let's save that issue for another day—perhaps when I find a philosopher to argue with you. I am only a poor doctor and scientist, no match for a philosopher in abstract matters.

Socrates: But about the matter you *do* know something of—we have still not found a morally relevant difference between fetus and infant, have we?

Herrod: Not yet. Except that the fetus is inside the mother, and the infant is outside.

Socrates: But we agreed that environmental mobility was not a morally relevant factor, did we not? (My, how I have slipped into jargon!) And you recall what happened when we explored the "part of the mother" argument, do you not?

Herrod: Yes. A big waterfall, with rocks on the bottom. Where shall we turn? Wait! Perhaps the very boat that took us downstream will take us up; perhaps the very fact that seems to count against me will count for me. I mean the fact that there is no sharp line. It's a matter of degree, a gradual process, becoming a person. Oh, no; that won't work. We already refuted that. It would mean that it was worse to kill a seventeen-year-old than a ten-year-old. . . . But either there is a sharp break, and then abortion after that is murder, or else there is not, and then it is not so bad to kill a ten-year-old as a seventeen-year-old. . . oh, dear! My boat seems to have hit a whirlpool. I must find the

Is birth the distinguishing point?

break. It must be at birth. But we went through that: none of the four differences count, and the "part of the mother" argument ended in absurdity. Hmmm .. suppose we compromise a bit and push personhood back into the womb a little. Let's try viability. What's wrong with saying that to be a person you must be viable independent of your mother?

Socrates: Let us examine this, then.

Herrod: I do not have much hope of escaping my whirlpool.

Socrates: Your twistings and turnings in the whirlpool may not be as hopeless as you think.

Does viability make a fetus human?

Herrod: But I am surrounded by difficulties!

Socrates: Did I ever promise you freedom from difficulties? Difficulties are the master's bait. But let us explore viability—that means the ability to live on its own, does it not?

Herrod: Yes.

Socrates: In other words, independence.

Herrod: Yes.

Socrates: Do you not see a number of problems here?

Herrod: All right, what are they? Please make it fast; my coffee's finished, and so am I, I think.

Socrates: For one thing, we have already rejected degree of dependence, one of the four differences we found between fetus and infant, as a difference between killing and murder. Two: the fetus is not dependent on the mother for its *identity*, its individuality. It has its own genetic code. Three: its dependence on the mother for nourishment and thus life continue long after birth. If dependence makes for nonpersons, small children are nonpersons and killing them is not murder. Four: the sick and elderly are dependent too; are they not persons? Five: all of us are always dependent: on each other, on nature.... Six: ...

Viability = independence

Dependence does not make a nonperson.

Herrod: Enough, already! Forget dependence. Let's not define viability simply as dependence. That's too vague. Viability is the ability to live outside the womb. If a fetus can be born and survive, let it be a person; if not, not.

Socrates: Well, now, let us investigate your new definition.

Herrod: Don't you ever leave anything alone?

Socrates: Of course not. Why should I?

Herrod: Don't you ever take a rest?

Socrates: We need rest from labor. This is not labor.

Herrod: It is for me.

Socrates: Then let us see whether this latest labor of yours is to be aborted or not. Tell me, please: does personhood depend on time and place?

Herrod: What do you mean?

Socrates: Do I cease to be a person when I leave a place or enter it?

Herrod: Of course not.

Socrates: And were people 2400 years ago less persons than people today?

Herrod: Of course not. What are you getting at?

Socrates: So personhood does not depend on time or place?

Herrod: Not in that sense, no.

Socrates: Now tell me another thing: is it not true that a baby that could live apart from its mother only with the aid of an incubator would not survive if there were no incubator?

Herrod: Of course.

Socrates: And there were no incubators 2400 years ago. Nor are there any in the wilderness.

Herrod: No.

Socrates: So a baby that is viable in the city may not be viable in the wilderness, and a baby that is viable today would not have been viable 2400 years ago.

Herrod: By the definition of viability we have used, that is correct.

Viability depends on time and place; personhood does not.
Socrates: Well, now, if personhood does not depend on time or place, and viability does depend on time or place, then viability cannot be the universal mark of personhood.

Herrod: Oh. That does follow, doesn't it? If we grant both the premises.

Socrates: Can you refute either one?

Herrod: No. But Socrates, this is all nit-picking and pettifoggery. Whenever a person begins, it just can't be as early as fertilization. Just look at that zygote: a single cell with no brain, no nervous system, no consciousness, no heart, no face—don't you feel the utter absurdity of calling *that* a human being?

Socrates: Because it doesn't look at all like a human being?

Herrod: Of course.

Socrates: But our question is not what it looks like but what it *is*.

Herrod: I'm not convinced there's any way to tell what a thing is except by observation of what it looks like.

Socrates: Do you mean to say that appearance and reality are the same? If so, why must we question appearances to find realities? If not, might this be a case where appearances are deceiving?

Herrod: But the reality seems so apparent here. Just look at the zygote. Doesn't it just feel silly to call that a person?

Socrates: Let us look, indeed; but feeling is not looking. Feeling is not the master's staff, is it?

Herrod: I don't believe we can discount feeling altogether. Feeling is part of our humanity too.

Socrates: Yes, but it is not the master's staff, is it? It is not able to see and thus to lead us. It has a heart but not an eye.

Herrod: Well, I have eyes. Let me tell you what I see.

Socrates: Fine, though I hope you also see with the x-ray eyes of the mind, and not only the external eyes of the senses.

Herrod: But we have to begin with the senses, at any rate. What do we see in the zygote? No differentiation of cells or functions or systems; no organs, no consciousness.

Socrates: True. It certainly is not an adult human being. But are you not confusing the question of

How could a single-celled zygote be a person?

What it looks like vs. what it is

whether it is a human being at all with the question of how developed a human being it is? Just a moment ago you were confusing the question of whether it is a human being with the question of whether it looks like a human being. Those are three different questions: what is it? what is its appearance? and what stage of growth has it attained? If it is not a human being, what is it? an ape? a fish?

Herrod: I'm willing to admit that it is a potential human being, not a potential ape or fish, but all its actuality remains unrealized, still in the future.

Socrates: Not *all* its actuality, or it would be nothing. To find out what it already is in actuality, let us look more closely at this useful distinction of yours. This business of the actualization of inherent potential—it seems to belong to the very nature of every living, growing thing, does it not?

Herrod: Yes indeed.

Socrates: So that we could call growth a kind of unfolding, could we not? An unfolding of already-present potential?

Herrod: Yes.

Socrates: And is not the zygote simply the first stage of this unfolding? It has almost all its growth or unfolding ahead of it, while the rest of us have some behind us and some ahead of us, and at the moment of death we have all of it behind us and no more ahead, at least on this earth?

Herrod: Yes, but then we are back to the gradual process: we never *are* fully actual, fully human. It is a matter of degree.

Socrates: What is a matter of degree? Maturity, not essence. A child is potentially adult, but not potentially human, don't you agree? Its potential is not to become a different species or essence, but a potential to unfold the essence. The essence is already there, guiding the unfolding.

Herrod: It seems to be, yes.

Socrates: And this seems to be true even of the zygote. Why else would every human zygote develop in human form, not as ape or anything else?

Herrod: There's no mystery about that, Socrates. We need not introduce invisible essences and potentialities. It's simply genetic programming.

Socrates: In that case, are we not back where we were a while ago, with the only radical break coming when a genetically new individual is formed, at conception?

Herrod: But you can't define a human being by mere genetics.

Socrates: If not by philosophical principles like essence or species and not by scientific principles like genetics, then by what *do* we define a human being?

Herrod: Maybe we can't define a human being at all. Maybe the whole question of the beginning of human life is a theological question, not a scientific one.

Is humanness a theological question?

Socrates: Did you hear that, Galileo?

Herrod: What? Who are you talking to?

Socrates: Oh, just an old friend of mine whom I met in another place and time—one with a fate and a sense of irony akin to my own. Look here. Will you look carefully with me at this moment, the act of conception, or fertilization, so that we may ascertain the facts on which to build any conclusions we may come to?

Herrod: Oh, all right.

Socrates: Good news, Galileo; he *will* look through your telescope!

Herrod: What?

66
The
Unaborted
Socrates

*What
happens
at
conception?*

Socrates: I'm sorry; I forgot that you cannot see him. Back to our data. Please tell me: what happens to the zygote immediately following fertilization?

Herrod: A kind of explosion or replication of cells.

Socrates: And what principle guides that replication? Where do these billions of complex designs come from?

Herrod: Are you going to try to bring God into it now?

Socrates: Well, I don't know; I hadn't planned to. Do *you* want to?

Herrod: Of course not.

Socrates: Oh. I thought you did.

Herrod: Why?

Socrates: Because you insisted that the question of when human life begins was a theological question. But tell me, these bits of information which guide the cell's development, are they the mother's genetic code?

Herrod: No.

Socrates: The father's?

Herrod: No.

Socrates: Whose, then, if not the new individual of the species homo sapiens?

Herrod: I don't know.

Socrates: Come now, Doctor. You know more science than that.

Herrod: Forget it. I give up. I have failed.

Socrates: We are trying *not* to forget—remember? And I think that instead of failing you have succeeded in taking the first steps. But will you look just a minute more at this moment of conception—this time from a philosophical point of view, just to be complete and join philosophy to science?

Herrod: I don't care.

Socrates: It seems you are getting tired. I shall make it as short as possible. Tell me, why do you suppose it is called conception?

Herrod: I don't know. You tell me, if you really want to make it short.

Socrates: I will tell you, but I will also wait for your approval before proceeding further. Is it not true that biological conception is very similar to mental conception, so that one is probably named after the other? I am thinking especially of the sudden moment of understanding. It is prefaced by preparatory steps of understanding and followed by other steps as well; but the moment of first understanding is a sudden and new thing—the moment when you say, "Aha!" Does it not seem as if we have a nice parallel in the world of the mind for what happens in the world of the womb? A really new thing, a radical break, a single moment of change at which we can reasonably draw a line and say something new has come into being?

Both biological and mental conception produce something radically new.

Herrod: If you like. Hmmph! I should have known from the beginning that you were one of *them.*

Socrates: One of *them*? Humans, you mean? Indeed. I too began as a zygote. Didn't you? And as you say, you should have known that from the beginning.

Herrod: You're toying with me. That's not what I meant and you know it.

Socrates: What do you mean then?

Herrod: I thought you were on my side. But you not only failed to find my defense; you became my accuser.

Socrates: How did I do that?

Herrod: By raising all those difficulties. Why do you

make difficulties everywhere? You sniff for diffi-culties like a pig snuffling for truffles—as if they were some delicacy. I think you are just a troublemaker.

Socrates: Oh, dear, that accusation sounds disturb-ingly familiar. Perhaps I can explain my method to you, as I could not explain it to my accusers many centuries ago. Look here: when you hunt a deer or a rabbit, do you search in the open spaces or in the bushes?

Herrod: In the bushes, of course.

Socrates: Why?

Herrod: Because that's where the animal is most likely to hide.

*Because
they are
the cover
where
truth
hides*

Socrates: Precisely. And I hunt not deer or rabbit but a far more valuable quarry, and a more elusive one: truth. And I have found my quarry hiding in a thicket of difficulties more often than not. Will you explore the bushes some more with me?

Herrod: No. It's getting late, and I'm tired and hun-gry.

Socrates: I am hungry too, but for a different food, I think. Have you nothing more to say in your de-fense, then? You realize the seriousness of the charge: nothing less than murder? And the strength of the testimony against you, the testimony of the common master and his instrument, the argument?

Herrod: I have one last thing to say, Socrates. They say a good offense is the best defense. Well, here is my last and best defense. You complimented me on a number of occasions for my hesitations and changes of mind, when I realized that I did not know. Should you not also blame my accusers for being dogmatic because they claim to know?

*Is it
foolish to
claim to
know when
human life
begins?*

Socrates: May I remind you again...

Herrod: I know, they are not here. But their accusation is. We have been sparring with it all afternoon, as with an arrow from the bow of some absent archer, some invisible opponent.

Socrates: Very well, let us make the arrow as visible as we can, though the archer is not here.

Herrod: They claim to know what they really do not know: that the fetus is a human person from the moment of conception.

Socrates: And you do you claim to know that it isn't?

Herrod: No. There is my advantage and my wisdom. I do not claim to know what I do not know. They do. They are the dogmatists. Theologians and philosophers and scientists have argued about this for many years without agreeing. It is sheer dogmatism for anyone to claim certainty about such a moot point. Even Thomas Aquinas taught that the fetus became human only in the third month of pregnancy. He thought the soul was "infused" into the body only then. So he said abortion was not murder until the third month.

Socrates: Thomas Aquinas did not know about genetics, did he?

Herrod: No. He lived back in the Dark Ages.

Socrates: The age of Gothic cathedrals, illuminated manuscripts, Dante, Marco Polo, universities, and courtly love poetry, you mean?

Herrod: Hmmph. *Scientifically* it was an age of ignorance.

Socrates: If Aquinas had known the genetics we know, do you think he would have allowed abortion before the third month?

Herrod: Perhaps not. But I brought him up only to

show that the issue is controversial. We simply do not know when the fetus becomes a human person. Anyone who claims to know is a fool because he claims to know what he does not know. Surely you above all men should be suspicious of that foolishness, Socrates. Didn't you classify everyone into two classes, the wise who know they are foolish and the foolish who think they are wise?

Socrates: Oh, I don't think I ever said anything quite as wise as that—although I should certainly applaud anyone who said it.

Herrod: Well, applaud, then. I just said it.

Socrates: Gladly. (Applauds.)

Herrod: Stop. You're attracting attention. You know, you can be very embarrassing.

Socrates: Why do you endure my presence then?

Herrod: Frankly, I thought I sensed a kindred soul. You too are a doctor—a doctor of the disease of claiming to know what you do not know—are you not?

Socrates: Yes, I try to treat that disease wherever I find it. The only question here is, where *do* we find it?

Herrod: Oh, I know where to find that disease, all right. My opponents are full of it.

Socrates: You *know* where to find that disease, do you?

Herrod: I think you are tripping me up in my words. But isn't it quite clear that they claim to know more than I do? They say they know the fetus is a person; I do not. So they are the fools for claiming to know, and I am wise for not claiming to know. Is that not clear?

Socrates: That remains to be seen. Shall we look?

Herrod: What is there to look at?

Who is it that is foolishly dogmatic?

Socrates: Your claim to be wise in knowing that you do not know.

Herrod: What remains to be seen in that claim?

Socrates: Let's see. You do not know whether the fetus is a person, correct?

Herrod: Correct.

Socrates: And your work here is to kill fetuses, correct?

Herrod: Socrates, I am continually shocked by the language you choose to use. I abort unwanted pregnancies.

Socrates: By killing fetuses or by something else?

Herrod: (Sigh.) By killing fetuses.

Socrates: Not knowing whether they are persons or not?

Herrod: Oh. Well...

Socrates: You said a moment ago that you did not know when the fetus became a person. Do you know now?

Herrod: No.

Socrates: Then you kill fetuses, not knowing whether they are persons or not?

Herrod: If you must put it that way.

Socrates: Now what would you say of a hunter who shot at a sudden movement in a bush, not knowing whether it was a deer or a fellow hunter? Would you call him wise or foolish?

Like a hunter shooting at an unidentified object

Herrod: Are you saying I am a murderer?

Socrates: I am only asking one question at a time. Shall I repeat the question?

Herrod: No.

Socrates: Then will you answer it?

Herrod: (Sigh.) All right. Such a hunter is foolish, Socrates.

Socrates: And why is he foolish?

Herrod: You never stop, do you?

Socrates: No. Wouldn't you say he is foolish because he claims to know what he does not know, namely, that it is only a deer and not his fellow hunter in the bush?

Herrod: I suppose so.

Or like an exterminator who fails to evacuate

Socrates: Or suppose a company were to fumigate a building with a highly toxic chemical to kill some insect pests, and you were responsible for evacuating the building first. If you were unsure whether there were any people left in the building and you nevertheless gave the order to fumigate the building, would that act be wise or foolish?

Herrod: Foolish, of course.

Socrates: Why? Is it not because you would be acting as if you knew something you really did not know, namely, that there were no people in the building?

Herrod: Yes.

The abortionist kills fetuses, not knowing whether they are human beings.

Socrates: And now you, Doctor. You kill fetuses—by whatever means, it does not matter; it may as well be by a gun or a poison. And you say that you do not know whether they are human persons. Is this not to act as if you knew what you admit you do not know? And is that not folly—in fact, the height of folly, rather than wisdom?

Herrod: I suppose you want me to meekly say "Yes indeed, Socrates. Anything you say, Socrates."

Socrates: Can you defend yourself against the argument?

The argument has devoured the abortionist.

Herrod: No.

Socrates: It has indeed devoured you like a shark, as surely as you devour fetuses.

Herrod: I suppose you think the case is closed.

Socrates: Not if you have any other lines of defense for us to examine. You mentioned many other aspects you wanted to discuss: women's rights, and the law, for instance. Will you return tomorrow and continue to examine your life's work with me? Do you not agree that "the unexamined life is not worth living"?

Herrod: Of course I shall be here tomorrow. This is my place of work. But wait. I have an idea. I have a friend who is a philosopher. He is in town for a convention. Perhaps he could help me answer your questions. In fact, he is giving a speech tomorrow at the convention on just this thing—abortion. Could you come to hear him? We could talk afterward.

Socrates: I would be very pleased to meet him. It is as I predicted in my *Apology:* even after my death I am to continue conversing with the philosophers. I never dreamed then that it included *future* philosophers as well as past. But then, the gods always exceed our expectations.

Herrod: I do not believe in gods.

Socrates: Perhaps we can talk about that too some time.

Herrod: My friend is a professor in a theological seminary. He also does not believe in gods.

Socrates: I met someone like that a while ago. He was a Christian Scientist, and he taught physical chemistry.

Herrod: I don't see the connection.

Socrates: Neither did he. But, then, many psychologists do not believe in the soul, the psyche. We must let those issues pass for now, since you are tired. I shall come to this convention tomorrow. Until then, good-bye, Doctor Herrod.

Herrod: Good-bye, Doctor Socrates.

DIALOG TWO
SOCRATES AT A PHILOSOPHY CONVENTION

time: *the second day*
place: *a convention hall in Athens*

dramatis personae:
Socrates
Dr. Rex Herrod, abortionist
Professor Attila Tarian, ethicist

Socrates: This is wrong.

Herrod: I beg your pardon, sir?

Socrates: Oh. I was talking to myself. I think I must be in the wrong place. I was supposed to meet someone at a philosophers' convention, but I seem to have stumbled on the slave market instead.

A philosophy convention or a slave market?

Herrod: This is the convention, all right, though some call it a slave market.

Socrates: The slaves, no doubt?

Herrod: Yes. Are you job hunting too?

Socrates: No. I have job security.

Herrod: I see I suppose you are not a philosopher?

Socrates: But I am.

Herrod: How did you get job security?

Socrates: The way any true philosopher gets it.

Herrod: Oh, you mean publishing?

Socrates: I never published a word in my life.

Herrod: Remarkable! How did you get tenure then?

The way to job security

Socrates: I didn't say I had tenure. I said I had job security.

Herrod: How did you get it?

Socrates: By a very simple device that anyone can learn.

Herrod: This sounds like a major discovery. What is it?

Socrates: Simply that I never took fees for my teaching.

Herrod: Why not?

Socrates: Because I am a philosopher.

Herrod: So are most of these others milling around here.

Socrates: Do they take fees?

Herrod: Of course.

Socrates: Then they are not true philosophers.

Herrod: Are you serious? What right do you have to make that judgment?

Socrates: Perhaps I am half serious. And perhaps I can show you by what right I judge: the right of reason. Tell me—what is a philosopher?

Herrod: A lover of wisdom, according to the word's meaning.

A lover of wisdom

Socrates: And a lover of wisdom must be a lover?

Herrod: Yes.

Socrates: And a lover is an amateur, is he not?

Herrod: According to the meaning of the word, yes.

Socrates: And an amateur is not a professional?

Herrod: You're playing with words.

Socrates: A lover's motive is love, is it not?

Herrod: Yes.

Socrates: And a professional's motive is money?

Herrod: That need not be the *only* motive.

Socrates: Indeed not. He may enjoy what he is doing. But he seeks to gain money, does he not? That is why he is a professional, not an amateur.

Herrod: Yes.

Socrates: Then one who takes fees is not a true philosopher.

Herrod: What is he, then?

Socrates: What do we call a professional lover, one who sells the acts of love for a fee?

A lover for money

Herrod: A prostitute. Are you saying that a professional philosopher is an intellectual prostitute? What a harsh judgment on all these poor little scrabblers!

Socrates: The judgment is not mine but reason's. If you take offense, you must refute the argument.

Herrod: You sound like someone I once met. No, I don't buy your argument, and I can't believe you're serious.

Socrates: The serious-minded will take me seriously, and those with half a wit will see me as a half-wit, which I am.

Herrod: A buffoon, I should say.

Socrates: Buffoonery should be easily refuted, should it not?

Herrod: Yes.

Socrates: Well, then, can you refute the argument of this buffoon?

Herrod: No.

Socrates: Then if you cannot refute the argument and you nevertheless refuse to admit the conclusion, that can mean only one thing.

Herrod: What's that?

Socrates: That you do not serve the common master.

Herrod: Why, bless my soul! It's Socrates! I didn't recognize you in a business suit.

Socrates in a business suit

Socrates: I am disguised. But I will do as you ask, though only the gods can guarantee your request.

Herrod: What request?

Socrates: I bless thy soul, Doctor Herrod.

Herrod: I didn't mean it literally. I don't believe in the soul.

Socrates: I see. Is it your body that has this opinion about your soul?

Herrod: Socrates, wait. I don't want to get into a long argument with you about the soul.

Socrates: And I suppose it is your body that makes that choice?

Herrod: I refuse to be trapped into another dialog. And it seems to me a very harsh judgment to call all these teachers intellectual prostitutes.

Socrates: I do not say that all teachers who take pay are only prostitutes. But I do say that philosophy is a passion, not a job. In fact, if it is not a passion, the "job" of teaching it cannot be accomplished. That is the serious point behind my buffoonery.

Herrod: You know, Socrates, less agile minds might take your seriousness playfully and your play seriously. In another time, your style could have been dangerous.

Socrates: In another time, it was. Perhaps at all times, in different ways.

Herrod: Well, there is no way a philosopher is dangerous in our time.

Socrates: That is indeed a tragic commentary on your time.

Herrod: Oh. Well, I did not invite you to anything dangerous today, at any rate.

Socrates: We shall see.

Herrod: I only want you to meet my friend and hear him lecture on abortion. His name is Dr. Atilla Tarian. He is a philosopher.

Socrates: Does he take fees?

Herrod: Of course. He teaches philosophy. Are you still playing that game for your own amusement?

Socrates: No, for your instruction. And here is an instructive test for you. Tell me, how do you answer this argument? If your friend sells a product or a service, he is a merchant, a middleman—one who mediates between his customer, the learner, and his product, wisdom. Would you agree?

Herrod: Yes. What is wrong with that?

Socrates: Must not a merchant deprive both producer and consumer, between whom he is the middleman?

Herrod: What! Why?

Socrates: Because unless he raises the price for the consumer and lowers the price for the producer, he makes no profit for himself.

Herrod: That's true. I never thought...

Socrates: That's true: you never thought. This is the essence of business. Now consider the essence of *successful* business. The more a businessman takes from both producer and consumer, the more successful he is. Does this not follow?

Herrod: I suppose so.

Is a teacher a merchant of ideas?

Socrates: Then please tell me why a teacher is not just such a merchant, one who deprives both his customer and his supplier as much as he can.

Herrod: Let me think about that question a moment, Socrates.

Socrates: Gladly. That is precisely my free service.

Herrod: Hmmm... look here. A teacher is different from a merchant because a teacher does not deal in material goods.

Socrates: An excellent answer. But a moment ago you were denying the existence of the soul. If there is no immaterial soul, whose goods are these immaterial goods?

Herrod: I don't know.

Socrates: But here is something you surely must know. What is the difference between material goods and immaterial goods?

Herrod: I must know that, must I?

Immaterial goods not diminished by sharing

Socrates: I think so. You know, do you not, that all material things, and money itself, the medium of exchange for them, diminishes the more it is shared?

Herrod: What do you mean?

Socrates: If I give you some of my money, I have less left to myself, do I not?

Herrod: Of course.

Socrates: But is wisdom similarly diminished by

sharing it? If I teach you, do I become less wise?
Herrod: Why, no. What a simple point, yet I never realized it before.
Socrates: That is part of my free service. Now tell me, is wisdom a good thing?
Herrod: Yes.
Socrates: Is it a material thing?
Herrod: No.
Socrates: Then it is an immaterial good. So there are immaterial goods.
Herrod: I suppose so.
Socrates: Goods *of* what, please?
Herrod: Of a human being.
Socrates: Of the body?
Herrod: Of the brain, which is part of the body, yes.
Socrates: The brain is material, is it not?
Herrod: Yes.
Socrates: Can you tell me how an immaterial good can reside in a material thing?
Herrod: Socrates, I did not come here to argue philosophy.
Socrates: That's a pity. It *is* a philosophy convention, you know.
Herrod: I see you're starving for your favorite food, syllogism sandwiches. Maybe later. But let's first listen to my friend Attila's lecture.
Socrates: All right. What is this convention, by the way?
Herrod: It's the International Convention of the Interdisciplinary Conference of Legal and Ethical Societies —I.C.I.C.L.E. for short.
Socrates: I see. And as befits your name, you are professionals.
Herrod: What do you mean?

Is wisdom an immaterial good of a material thing?

I.C.I.C.L.E.

Socrates: Are you hot-blooded youth passionately pursuing wisdom as your adored beloved? Or are you cold-hearted professionals dickering for a price in the marketplace—icicles, one may say?

Herrod: That's a good pun, Socrates, but I must be businesslike about the time. Attila is about to give his speech. He's defending the very thing we were arguing about yesterday: abortion. Since my work is at stake and since I could not defend it adequately yesterday, I want you to come with me to hear him. He will put up a much stronger case than I did, I'm sure. He is a philosopher.

Socrates: So you said. Will he allow me to cross-examine him afterward? You see, I learn little from speeches, unless I can ask questions, as befits a learner and a beginner. If this man is a true teacher, as you say he is, he should not mind teaching me by answering my questions.

Herrod: I'm sure he will. Here—the speech is in this room. Why do people keep staring at you?

Socrates: Perhaps they have seen my face in statuary, or the face of my archetype, Silenus, and they now recollect. All learning is recollection, you know.

Herrod: I seem to recollect that. Ah, here we are. Let's sit in the last row so that we don't call attention to ourselves. There's Attila coming out of the men's room.

Socrates: You mean so that *I* don't call attention to us. Life would be so much simpler if people just said what they meant.

Herrod: Listen. He's beginning.

Tarian: Ladies and gentlemen, my speech has already been handed out in printed form, so rather than reading it now, I would like to summarize its five main points and reserve the remaining time for questioning.

Socrates: A promising beginning. How fortunate that I have studied your entire library and understand the barbarous tongue he speaks: English, is it not?

Herrod: Yes. Listen.

Tarian: First a word about myself and where I'm coming from.

Socrates: I know where he's coming from. I just saw him coming from the men's room.

Herrod: Shhh.

Tarian: I am arguing in this paper for more liberal abortion laws. Although I am not a lawyer but a philosopher—an ethicist—I have chosen this legal topic because I regard practical legal issues as tests for abstract philosophical principles. I distrust abstract philosophy that is not tested in concrete, lived situations. As you know, I have defended ethical relativism, situationism and utilitarianism against absolutism and abstract principialism. My paper is an attempt to apply that philosophy to the issue of liberal abortion laws. I have five reasons to support my conclusion.

The first is that as a matter of historical fact most of the opposition to abortion has been and continues to be based on religious foundations. The leading proponent of restrictive abortion laws is the Roman Catholic Church. This is a bald power play, an attempt to impose the morality of one group on all others by force, thus endangering the freedom of choice on which the modern democratic state is founded.

I favor a tolerant and pluralistic society. Here, I believe, is modernity's chief claim to superiority over the ancients. We are as pro-choice as possible in every

Five reasons for liberal abortion laws: (1) Opposition to abortion is ecclesiastical.

area; we love freedom. We restrict minimally. We are, however, restrictive about restrictions. We restrict any one group's plans to restrict other groups. Liberal abortion laws do not restrict conservatives—no one wants to force anyone to get an abortion—but conservative abortion laws do restrict liberals. Conservatives want to force everyone *not* to have abortions.

(2) You can't legislate morality

My second reason concerns the relation between law and morality. Just as it has been the genius of the modern state to separate State and Church, we also rightly distinguish law and morality. The purpose of law is not to make people virtuous, as poor old Plato thought. We do not try to legislate morality, for the very good reason that the thing simply cannot be done. Morality must be free, not compelled by law. Unless a choice is free, it cannot be a moral choice. But law necessarily involves sanction, threat of punishment for disobedience. This is compulsion, not freedom. Law, then, is the very antithesis of morality. The term *moral law* is a confusion. Abortion is indeed a moral issue, a free, personal decision; and for that reason it should not be taken from the freedom of the individual and decided by law.

(3) Restrictive abortion laws are unenforceable.

My third reason is a purely practical one: laws restricting abortions are simply unenforceable. Women who want abortions will get them one way or another. The only choice is between illegal, dangerous, back-alley, coat-hanger abortions or legal, safe, regulated abortions. I believe it was a maxim of legal philosophers that "an unenforceable law cannot bind."

(4) Every child a wanted child

A fourth point could be summarized by the slogan: Every Child a Wanted Child. Surely this seems to be an ethical ideal if anything is: a world in which every person who is born is loved and wanted. Here is the strength of an ethic of consequences and the weakness of an ethic of abstract principles: the former leads to a better, happier world than the second.

My fifth point could be summarized by the phrase "an ethic of compassion." We are unlike the ancients, who thought it ethically good to endure terrible sufferings and to invite or even demand those sufferings of others—supposedly to train the soul. We value compassion and the *relief* of suffering. Would it not then be highly *un*ethical to demand of thousands, even millions, of pregnant women a degree of suffering which some would call heroic sanctity (if sanctity it be to suffer at the hands of the uncompassionate)? In any case it is certainly not sanctity to *be* uncompassionate.

(5) An ethic of compassion

Having summarized my five reasons very sketchily, I now invite questions from the audience. Yes, the little man in the back row.

Socrates: We are speaking of laws here. May I ask a question about the laws of procedure?

Tarian: Certainly.

Socrates: Is one allowed to question everything you have said?

Tarian: Yes, of course.

Socrates: Then have the servants provided ample food and drink for this enterprise?

Tarian: What do you mean?

Socrates: We are speaking of justice here. Surely to do even a little justice to the investigation of even one of the reasons you have given will require a great deal of leisure.

Tarian: (Stiffly): We have a ten-minute time limit. Questioners are requested to confine their remarks

Socrates asks about time.

to two minutes each.

Socrates: Oh, dear. It is indeed as the myths say: Kronos is the cruellest of all tyrants, until one learns to live instead under Kairos...

Tarian: Sir, could we just have your question, please?

Socrates: I'm sorry. I am not a subject of your master. I shall instead hope for another time, fit for free men rather than slaves—a time of leisure when we can eat and drink both food and words together. I should have known; someone described this convention as a slave market. I did not realize until now who the master was.

Tarian: Sir, the situation compels us...

Socrates: Yes, I see. Your master has many names.

Tarian: What do you mean?

Socrates: Kronos and Situation are two of them. From the first part of your speech I suspect that History is a third, though others have called her the strumpet Fortune.

Tarian: Perhaps later... we could talk at length some other time.

Socrates: Thank you. Whenever your master frees you.

Tarian: Harrumph! Uh... are there... ah... any other questions? I mean, any *real* questions? To me, I mean, not to the man in the back row... no? Oh.

Uh... yes. Well... uh... thank you anyway. Thank you. Thank you. Good day.

Herrod: You confused and embarrassed him. Look. Everyone is laughing at him. They want to ask *you* questions now.

Socrates: I'm truly sorry. I didn't mean it to come to that. I should apologize. Oh, good; here he comes. To see you, I think.

Tarian: Rex, old buddy. How good to see you! And this new friend of yours is just as odd as you said he was. Good day to you, sir. I'm sorry we could not dialog before.

Socrates: Good day to you, sir. It is I who am sorry for embarrassing you.

Tarian: Forget it. Herrod tells me you call yourself Socrates.

Socrates: Yes. And you call yourself Tarian.

Tarian: But do you really think you are Socrates?

Socrates: Do you really think you are Tarian?

Tarian: I guess I mean to ask: What do you want me to call you?

Socrates: My name, if you please. What do you want me to call *you*?

Tarian: You might call me a taxi. I'm not sure I want to stay.

Socrates: Well, then, you're a taxi. But please stay. I'm really quite harmless. All I want is some conversation.

Tarian: Well, I do want to meet you.

Socrates: You already have.

Tarian: Yes. Indeed. Say, is there a place we can go? We seem to be drawing a crowd.

Socrates: I don't mind crowds. Do you?

Tarian: The situation is becoming intolerable. They're laughing at us.

Socrates: Is it not an act of impiety against your god to try to alter him?

Tarian: What? What do you mean?

Socrates: The Situation, formerly your master, has now become your servant.

Tarian: Hmmm...

Herrod: Look here. Through one of these doors is a

Tarian meets Socrates.

Through the door into the garden

small, private garden. A wonderful spot for a conversation, don't you think?

Socrates: Appropriate, I should say. Every good conversation creates its own inward garden in the soul.

Tarian: The soul. Well, now, that's a tricky concept to chew on.

Herrod: Before you two get off on soul food, let's try this door. Ah, here it is. How's this?

Socrates: Charming.

Tarian: The situation is improving.

Socrates: What a changeable god!

Herrod: Let's lock the door behind us so the crowd can't follow. Now—how shall we begin?

Socrates: Dr. Tarian, may I question each part of your speech now?

Tarian: Yes. And Rex, could we have the king play the part of the servant today? Would you go get us something to drink?

Herrod: Glad to. What would you like?

Tarian: Whiskey.

Socrates: I'll have some wine, if you please. Tell me, Professor Tarian, did Dr. Herrod tell you of our conversation yesterday?

Tarian: Yes. In fact, he made a tape of it and played it for me. He hoped you wouldn't mind.

Socrates: Why would I mind? I made my own "tape," called memory. You know, it's quite remarkable how you moderns have invented the external mind with all your libraries and tape recorders and microfilm and computers. I wonder that your internal mind does not become weak and flabby, like a newly rich master who lets his slaves do all his work. But let us get on to your first point. Tell me, did you notice any religious reasons given for any of our arguments on the

*Tarian's
first
objection:
opposition
to abortion
is
ecclesiastical.*

tape you listened to?

Tarian: No. Actually, the question came up a couple of times, whether the question of abortion was theological, and you both decided that it was not.

Socrates: And were any of the arguments against abortion based on religious premises?

Tarian: No.

Socrates: Your recall is correct. Science provided the facts about the fetus and philosophy provided the principles about murder. Why do you think the issue is a religious issue?

Tarian: Tell me, why do *you* think the Catholic Church is in the forefront of the antiabortion cause?

Socrates: I had always assumed that it was because the Church thought abortion was murder and was defending the rights of the victims.

Tarian: And why do you think they want to force their beliefs on non-Catholics?

Socrates: I had thought it was because there were so many non-Catholic victims.

Tarian: Don't be naive, Socrates. It's a power play.

Socrates: It seems likely to me that it is you who are naive here. For to close the mind to the possibility of a proper motive is as naive and simple-minded as to close the mind to the possibility of an improper motive. Does not the motive here seem to be the same as that behind the Church's opposition to racism, slavery, war, child abuse and the like?

Tarian: And why do you think that the Church's voice is raised so much louder and more hysterically against abortion than against those other tragedies?

Socrates: *Tragedies,* you call them? In my culture a tragedy meant a drama of a good man with a flaw suffering his necessary fate.

None of the arguments against abortion were religious.

Tarian: Evils, then. Wrongs. Why doesn't the Church oppose poverty as strongly as it opposes abortion? That causes much more suffering. The Church seems pretty selective in its moral outrage.

Socrates: I suppose it's because speaking against poverty does very little actual good, for the poverty is already there; the thing to do is to relieve it. But speaking against abortion may do much good by deterring someone from committing it. Abortion is committed; poverty is only endured. Abortion is a moral evil; poverty is a physical one (though its *cause* may be a moral evil). The Church's opposition, as I understand it, is not so much to suffering as to sin. Poverty and pain and illness and even death are not sins, though they may have been caused by sin. They are evil only to the body, not to the soul. Sin affects the soul.

Abortion a moral evil, poverty a physical evil

Tarian: The soul again!

Socrates: Yes. You see, I happen to understand this point of view because I made the discovery long ago that the true self is the soul, and the soul's harm comes from vice and ignorance and sin, not from suffering or even death of the body.

Tarian: Could we get from this pious idealism back to the issue?

Socrates: Oh, but this is the issue. The issue is the harm in abortion, and the greatest harm is not to the body of the victim but to the soul of the perpetrator. Abortion harms the mother more than the fetus.

Abortion harms the mother more than the fetus.

Tarian: Ridiculous!

Socrates: Is there such a thing as a person's character?

Tarian: Yes...

Socrates: Is this valuable?

Tarian: Yes.

Socrates: More valuable than the body?

Tarian: I can't compare apples with oranges.

Socrates: Would you rather be crippled in character or in body?

Tarian: I can't decide such a question.

Socrates: Would you rather be a sadistic torturer of martyrs, or a martyred victim of a sadistic torturer?

Tarian: What a terrible choice! I can't decide.

Socrates: Decide this, then. Suppose your son were a soldier captured by a cruel enemy and asked to torture his fellow prisoners or else be a victim of torture. Which would you hope for him to choose?

Tarian: Another terrible situation! Why must you ask me this?

Socrates: To find out which you would choose—situationally, if you please. In that situation, which choice is less evil?

Tarian: What are you trying to prove?

Socrates: That you too recognize the fact that doing evil is worse than suffering it—for those you love, at least, if not for yourself. You may label it pious idealism for yourself, but do you not hope your son proves to be a "pious idealist" and suffers evil rather than doing it?

Doing evil is worse than suffering it.

Tarian: That sounds nice. But it's really very nasty, if you mean to apply it to abortion. It implies that all those millions of mothers, or their doctors, or both, have terribly evil characters. How judgmental you ethical absolutists are!

Socrates: It is not I but the argument that is the subject of the judgment, and it is not the criminal but the crime that is the object.

Tarian: What do you personally say about these so-called criminals, then?

Socrates: I suppose that most aborting mothers in an abortionist society do not fully realize the gravity of abortion. They are filched of their instinct for justice, for life, and for motherhood, and filched of their tradition as well.

Tarian: Filched? By whom?

Socrates: By the Sophists.

Tarian: Aren't you in the wrong century?

Socrates: It may be the century that is in the wrong.

Tarian: At least our century would not kill you for your ideas, as yours did.

Socrates: I was the only one in Athens who was killed for my ideas. How many people have been killed for their ideas in your century so far?

Tarian: Millions. But not here. This is not Russia or China or Iran. This is Greece. A democracy.

Socrates: Yes, I am somewhat familiar both with Greece and with democracy, you know. I happen to have been executed in Greece and in a democracy.

Tarian: Oh, yes, that's right, isn't it?

Socrates: No, that's wrong. But it happened.

Tarian: Hmmph. You were executed for not believing in the gods of the state, weren't you?

Socrates: Yes.

Tarian: Well, then, surely you should favor the separation of Church and State and tolerance of different religions and philosophies.

Socrates: Indeed I do.

Tarian: So your pupil Plato betrayed your position in the *Republic*.

Socrates: Alas, yes. It is even said that if I had appeared in Plato's realized Republic, I would have been executed a second time.

Tarian's second objection: tolerance ("you can't legislate morality")

Tarian: Then you are all for tolerance and the open society and freedom of thought. You agree that you can't legislate morality.

Socrates: Yes. But there must be some laws governing *deeds*, must there not? Some minimal restrictions on freedom of action, though none on freedom of thought?

Tarian: I couldn't have put it better myself.

Socrates: No, I don't think you could have.

Tarian: But this means we agree in principle. You are a liberal, like myself.

Socrates: Am I really? You know, I have been investigating this mysterious question of just who and what I am ever since the god who spoke through the Delphic oracle commissioned me to philosophize and his motto became mine. "Know thyself" indeed; but it is no easy task, and I am far from finished. So if you can help me to complete my god-given task by your category of "liberal" I shall be eternally grateful. But I must first understand what this category means, and this I have not been able to do.

What is a "liberal"?

Tarian: What's the mystery, Socrates? A liberal is just the opposite of a conservative.

Herrod: (Entering, with drinks.) And a conservative is a liberal who just got mugged.

Tarian: Oh, Rex. Thanks. For the drinks and for the definition. But couldn't you also say a liberal is a conservative who just got arrested?

Socrates: Perhaps the best definition is the one given by your wise wag Ambrose Bierce: "A conservative is enamored of existing evils; a liberal wants to replace them with new ones." But beyond the jest, I see no serious categories here, only two fishnet terms.

Tarian: What do you mean *fishnet terms*?

*The two
fishnet
terms:
liberal
and
conservative*

Socrates: Just that you modern people try to catch every idea that swims through the seas of your mind in one of two great fishnets labeled liberal and conservative so that you needn't think through each issue separately. What a wonderful feat of mental technology; what a labor-saving device for thought! But there is a problem with it: I seem to see hundreds of big and little fish swimming in and out through the holes in both nets.

Tarian: For instance?

Socrates: Take the class of issues we are discussing: issues about human life. Wouldn't you agree that logically there are two possibilities? Either human life is sacred, or not.

Tarian: Yes, and that old "sanctity of life" superstition is exactly the trouble here. Take the idea of "quality of life," on the other hand. Now that's a realistic concept...

*Two
classical
ethical
philosophies:
idealism
and
utilitarianism*

Socrates: Some other time we should argue that issue, for it seems no less than the issue between civilization and barbarism. But we differ on which side is barbaric. My only point now is to define the two sides, not to argue them. Is it not true that the ethical idealist says human life is sacred and the utilitarian says this is not so?

Tarian: Yes.

Socrates: Now let us look at the liberal and conservative fishnets. You liberals are against capital punishment, are you not?

Tarian: Yes.

Socrates: And strongly antiwar? You tend toward pacifism?

Tarian: Yes.

Socrates: And you want governments to help the

poor more?

Tarian: Yes.

Socrates: But you will tolerate abortion and euthanasia?

Tarian: Well... yes.

Socrates: On the other hand, your typical conservative opponent opposes abortion and euthanasia, but favors capital punishment and tends to be weak in opposing war and favoring help for the poor.

Tarian: Yes. They are the cold-hearted icicles. We are warm and compassionate. Surely you see the difference.

Socrates: Do you see any inconsistency in their position?

Tarian: I think so.

Socrates: I wonder whether it is the same one I see. Would you point it out?

Tarian: Gladly. Their "sanctity of life" ethic is two-faced. If life is sacred in the abortion clinic or the gerontology ward, why isn't it also sacred on the battlefield or in the prison or in the ghetto?

Socrates: A good question, Professor. And now may I ask you one? If life is sacred in the ghetto, on the battlefield, and in the prison, why is it not also sacred in the abortion clinic or the gerontology ward?

Tarian: Oh. I see your question. It seems I have only turned their inconsistency upside-down rather than escaping it.

Socrates: Exactly. Now can you explain to me how this is only a seeming?

Tarian: I think I can. You see, I just want governments to step back and not restrict individual free choice. I hate force. Forcing a woman to bear a child, forcing a prisoner to the electric chair, forcing a sol-

If life is sacred in the abortion clinic, why not also on the battlefield?

And vice versa

Justification of liberalism: individual choice

dier to die in battle—these are all cases of the same thing. Don't you agree that a society with only the necessary, minimal restrictions and laws is best?

Socrates: I do. So we must now find out just what these necessary, minimal restrictions and laws are, and then whether laws against abortion must be included in them. If we agree on the principle, perhaps we can deduce from it the correct conclusion about abortion laws.

Tarian: Oh, we will never agree about abortion laws, Socrates. You are naive if you think otherwise. It's all relative; different people have different opinions and always will.

"It is all relative."

Socrates: Just what is this "it" that is "all relative," please?

Tarian: Justice. What laws are just or good or right or proper or necessary. That sort of thing. What we've been talking about.

Socrates: I had hoped we were at least talking about one thing at a time. You just mentioned five. Do you have the patience to define these terms, so that we know what we are talking about?

Tarian: Frankly, no. The whiskey is half gone and so, I think, is our conversation. I'd rather not waste our remaining time on dull definitions.

Socrates: Oh, dear. I thought we had escaped the tyrant Kronos, but I see you are still chained to his hourglass. Are we still dependent on his dole of hours? Never mind. We can take the short road if you wish, though it is seldom as sure as the long one. Tell me, do you mean to say that in the realm of things just and unjust there are no absolutes and everything is relative?

Tarian: Exactly.

Socrates: Absolutely, in other words.

Tarian: What?

Socrates: There are absolutely no absolutes?

Tarian: That's just a verbal trick, Socrates.

Socrates: Indeed it is, but you are the trickster, not I. I merely revealed your own contradiction.

Tarian: Let's get down to concrete issues. In a state where people differ about justice and values, we need maximum tolerance, don't you agree?

Socrates: Yes. But we have not yet found how much tolerance is maximum and how much restriction is minimum. Would you tolerate the intolerant?

Tarian: Another verbal trick!

Socrates: Not at all, Professor. If a bully beat up your child, or if a tyrant took over your state and your freedom, would you tolerate these intolerant people?

Tarian: Of course not. That's where minimal laws come in. They protect freedom. Surely you agree with that.

Socrates: I do. Now don't liberal abortion laws allow some people to force death on the fetus?

Tarian: But the fetus is not a person.

Socrates: And once again we are back to the one and only foundational issue.

Tarian: No, here is my other issue. I'm against laws that take away a woman's freedom of choice to have or to terminate her pregnancy.

Socrates: Why? Because you don't want to force people?

Tarian: Exactly.

Socrates: But you would have the fetus forced to die.

Tarian: You keep assuming it is a person.

Socrates: And you keep assuming it is not. You see? That is the issue.

Tarian: There is also a legal issue and a political one. You want the State to force us to be virtuous, as you define virtue.

Socrates: I think you are confusing me with my pupil, Plato. Let's say I agree with your libertarian principles, at least for a modern, pluralistic state. What follows?

*Isn't
pro-choice
less
restrictive?*

Tarian: Pro-choicers don't want to force pro-lifers to have abortions, but pro-lifers do want to force pro-choicers not to have them. We don't want to restrict them, but they do want to restrict us. We are the true libertarians. Don't you see that? It's obvious.

Socrates: I do indeed see what you see. Whether you also see what I see, remains to be seen.

Tarian: What do you see?

Socrates: I see some who are much more severely restricted by liberal abortion laws than anyone is by conservative abortion laws.

Tarian: What? That's impossible.

Socrates: Abortion is possible, is it not?

Tarian: Of course . . .

Socrates: Then what about its millions of victims? Is it not the most severe restriction of all to be killed? If you are really against force, why do you want to force death on unwilling millions?

Tarian: You're treating the fetus as a person.

*It all
comes back
to the
issue of the
fetus.*

Socrates: And you're treating it as a nonperson. You see? Every argument logically comes back to that issue, which Dr. Herrod and I discussed yesterday.

Tarian: Suppose it does. Then, since we disagree about that issue, let us agree to differ, but let us not impose our values on each other.

Socrates: That is another of your favorite clichés that I have never been able to comprehend. Surely you do not mean that we should not try to convince each other of the truth of our beliefs?

Tarian: Why couldn't I mean just that? I don't like proselytism.

Socrates: If we honestly believe what we say is true, why should we deprive each other of this great good? Unless truth is not a good?

Tarian: Let me try to explain myself to you, Socrates. I think you're misjudging me. I'm not pro-abortion, you know, just pro-choice. I'm against abortion personally. But I don't want to impose my values on others by making it a matter of public law and compulsion rather than private choice and freedom. Surely you must understand that!

Socrates: Only if I try to understand it. And the only way I know to do that is by asking you questions about it.

Tarian: Ask away then.

Socrates: *Why* are you personally against abortion? Tell me, which of these three positions is yours: would you say a fetus is a human being, or not a human being, or don't you know?

Tarian: Why must you go back to that question now?

Socrates: Because if you think a fetus is a human being, you surely ought to protect it by law against its potential murderers, just as we protect all other human beings. But if you think it is not a human being, why are you personally against abortion? And if you don't know, mustn't you act on the chance that it *may* be a human being and not risk murder?

Tarian: It doesn't matter which of the three I choose. Whatever my own views are, I won't impose them on those who disagree with me.

Socrates: I think you would, if you believed they

*Even
minimal
laws must
protect the
innocent.*

*The parallel
with laws
against
lynching*

were true. Surely law should compel everyone to protect innocent human life, even if they do not want to, wouldn't you agree?

Tarian: I hate compulsion.

Socrates: That is indeed an interesting fact about your personal psychological makeup, but it is not an answer to my question. Let me put it more concretely. Suppose in your country the Ku Klux Klan wanted to begin lynching again. Lynching is a value to them, but not to you, is it not?

Tarian: You could put it that way, yes.

Socrates: Would you then be "imposing your values" on them by making and enforcing laws against lynching?

Tarian: That's not imposing my values. That's just ... just...

Socrates: What?

Tarian: I don't know.

Socrates: Oho!

Tarian: That's not fair—to jump on me just because I was honest enough to admit I need to think more about this.

Socrates: Oh, no, dear Professor. I was not jumping on you, but rather jumping for joy *for* you.

Tarian: You mean for yourself. You're winning the argument.

Socrates: No, Professor; for you. You see, I have discovered that those three precious little words you just said are the beginning of all wisdom, and I rejoice at your wisdom.

Tarian: What words?

Socrates: I don't know.

Tarian: If you don't even know what words they are, how do you know they are wise?

Socrates: I do know the words.

Tarian: What are the words?

Socrates: I don't know.

Tarian: You are an idiot!

Socrates: That is simply another, stronger, way of putting my point, yes. But let's get back to another example. Suppose a Neo-Nazi party arose and wanted to begin exterminating Jews again. Would you be imposing your values on them by restricting their activity?

The parallel with Nazism

Tarian: Of course not.

Socrates: What would you be doing?

Tarian: Restricting their activity, that's what.

Socrates: Touché; I must make the question clearer. What would justify this force on your part?

Tarian: Protecting the innocent.

Socrates: Precisely. And is not the anti-abortionist in exactly the same position?

Tarian: But Jews and Blacks are persons. A fetus is not.

Socrates: And so we are back once again to yesterday's issue. There is nothing new to say, then, is there?

Tarian: Yes there is. The cases are different.

Socrates: How, except for the question of whether the fetus is a person?

Tarian: Everyone admits that lynching and genocide are wrong, but there is a plurality of opinions about abortion.

Socrates: Everyone admits lynching and genocide are wrong? Including the Klan and the Nazis?

Tarian: Oh, well, no.

Socrates: And pro-abortionists also do not admit that abortion is wrong. There are two sides to each of the three issues. Where then is the difference?

Tarian: Pro-choice people are a large segment of society. The Klan and the Nazis are a handful.

Socrates: The Nazis were far more than a handful at one time. Was genocide right then? Can you decide right and wrong by force of numbers?

Tarian: Indeed you can, Socrates! That sounds wrong, but it's the principle of democracy: the majority rules.

Socrates: Is the majority always right?

Tarian: The majority in a democracy declares what is right.

Socrates: Can they make a mistake? Did the Nazis make a mistake?

Tarian: Of course *I* think so, but *they* did not.

Socrates: I am aware of that. But were they really wrong?

Tarian: I cannot make that judgment.

Socrates: But you just did, my good man. In answer to my question, did the Nazis make a mistake? you said, "I think so."

Tarian: By *my* standards.

Socrates: Are your standards merely yours, like your taste for olives? Are they not an attempt to understand any universal truths or goods about human nature or human rights?

Tarian: You're steering the argument into abstractions again.

Socrates: Then answer this concrete question, please: how in a democracy are minorities protected against majorities? If the majority agreed to make lynching "safe and legal," would it still be a good law to make it illegal?

Tarian: I think so, but the majority who voted for

lynching would not.

Socrates: I already know those two things, Professor. I am asking about a third thing. Perhaps you misunderstood my question. I did not ask you what you or they think but what is. A sociologist or psychologist can poll opinions; I am not asking you to be a sociologist now but a philosopher. Tell me not about your opinion but about the thing you opine, about good laws, about justice.

Tarian: Your philosophical question is impossible to answer. Justice is simply a matter of opinion.

Socrates: What subject do you teach, Professor? What do you profess?

Tarian: Philosophy.

Socrates: And philosophy, you say, asks questions that are impossible to answer. So you are a professor of the impossible.

Tarian: Consistency is the hobgoblin of little minds, Socrates.

Socrates: I see there is no danger of your being haunted by such goblins.

Tarian: The serious point is just that justice is only a matter of opinion.

Justice a matter of opinion?

Socrates: So an opinion about justice is an opinion about an opinion.

Tarian: I refuse to be trapped in your logical hall of mirrors.

Socrates: It is not mine, Professor; it is yours. It is your mind that is the hall of mirrors. All swept clean of goblins.

Tarian: I refuse to argue about abstractions.

Socrates: Do you also refuse to protect minorities against majorities?

Tarian: No. Now we're back in the real world.

Socrates: Then how do you protect them?

Tarian: By laws, of course.

Socrates: Laws you think just?

Tarian: Yes.

Socrates: But those same laws others think unjust.

Tarian: I doubt whether people like the Klan or the Nazis ever really care about justice.

Socrates: But if they claimed to care and insisted that their laws were just and yours were unjust, would you retract your repressive laws and allow lynching and genocide as they demanded?

Tarian: No.

Socrates: Not even if they became fifty-one per cent of the population?

Tarian: No. Not even then. I would fight against them.

Socrates: Why? What justifies your "imposing your values on others"?

Tarian: This is obviously a case of those minimal, necessary laws we spoke of.

Anti-abortion laws necessary to protect persons

Socrates: And anti-abortion laws are not necessary because a fetus is not a person?

Tarian: Yes. Back to yesterday's issue. Can we go home now?

Socrates: I would still like to understand your strange phrase *imposing my values on others.* Would such a law be imposing your values on others or not?

Tarian: What difference does it make which way I answer? It's only a question of words. You're great at tripping people up in their words. You'll win the argument either way I answer. The real point is not about words but about the real world.

Words vs. realities

Socrates: I fear I am losing the argument, because I am not getting what I wanted: an understanding of your words. But you are quite right: the real point is not words but the world. If you ever find my words not to be about the real world, please let me know, and I shall flee from them as from a ghost—or a hall of mirrors.

Tarian: Why do you use your famous dialectic all the time then?

Socrates: I find the real world so terribly logical that I use this instrument to reveal the world as best I can.

Tarian: Well, most people don't find the real world so "terribly logical." Tell me, what do you find so logical about bombs and inflation and rape and death?

Is the real world logical?

Socrates: That bombs are bombs, and that two million plus two million always make four million, and that every event has a cause, even rape, and that mortals are not immortal, and other astonishing paradoxes.

Tarian: Forget your silly paradoxes. My point is plain. I want compassionate laws, laws that help people, not repress them.

Socrates: Helping them by protecting them against bombs and inflation and rape?

Tarian: Yes.

Socrates: And against lynching and genocide?

Tarian: Yes.

Socrates: But not against abortion.

Tarian: I want to help *people*. It is real people who want abortions.

Socrates: And it is real people who want lynching and genocide and rape.

Tarian: But it is people who are being raped and lynched.

Socrates: And people who are being aborted.

Tarian: Back to yesterday's issue.

Back to issue #1

Socrates: Always. Do you have any refutation of it?

Tarian: Socrates, my head is getting confused with your dialectic. Please let's forget the logic and look at the facts instead.

Socrates: Instead?

But abortion is legal.

Tarian: Like it or not, the plain fact of the matter is that abortion is now legal in most countries. The American Supreme Court, for instance, has declared it legal.

Socrates: That same Supreme Court once decreed that a black slave was not a person, did it not?

Tarian: Yes.

Socrates: And Nazi laws decreed that Jews were in effect nonpersons.

Tarian: Yes.

Socrates: Surely you would say such laws were wrong?

Tarian: I don't like them, but others do.

Socrates: Again you give me psychology or sociology when I ask for philosophy. *Are* such laws wrong?

Right and wrong only opinions?

Tarian: I will not dogmatically assert that, no. It is a matter of opinion.

Socrates: Whether it is wrong to deliberately slaughter an entire race of people is a matter of opinion?

Tarian: Certainly. I will defend my opinion, but I will also defend everyone's right to his or her own opinion, however much I may disagree with it.

Socrates: Is it "certainly" true that this is only a matter of opinion? You are *not* certain that genocide is wrong, but you *are* certain that those who claim they *know* it is wrong, are wrong?

Tarian: Yes.

Are all opinions equal?

Socrates: Are all opinions equally true?

Tarian: All opinions must count. It is dogmatic to insist that only yours is true.

Socrates: So a madman's opinion must count as much as a sane man's? Barbarism has equal rights with civilization?

Tarian: One man's barbarism is another man's civilization. Who's to say who's sane and who's insane, anyway?

Socrates: You are, if you are an honest man. Do we not each have the duty to try to find the truth and say it? Do you refuse that duty?

Tarian: The truth, eh? And just what is that, anyway?

Socrates: That question reminds me of someone else I met nearly two thousand years ago.

Tarian: It's a rhetorical question, Socrates. A way of saying that truth is subjective, not objective.

Socrates: I see. Tell me, please, do you think this subjectivism of yours is really true? Or is it too only subjective? Are you only expressing how you feel, like a yawn or a belch?

Tarian: There is no need to be rude, Socrates.

Socrates: On the contrary, I think there is. When a thought is rude and barbaric, it is appropriate to treat it rudely. But I do not wish to substitute name-calling for logic. So please tell me: is your subjectivism objectively true?

Tarian: Do you think you can trap me that easily? Of course not. I claim only that it is true for me.

Socrates: I am not trying to trap you, my good man. On the contrary, I hold out the free choice between two logical alternatives in answer to every question. You see, I am truly pro-choice.

Tarian: But if I say there is no objective truth, you will say, "How do you know that? Is that an objective truth that you know? Is it true that there is no truth?"

What is Truth?

Is subjectivism objectively true?

Socrates: If I am as clever as you are, I might say that, yes. Thank you for so perfectly trapping yourself. Can you escape from your own trap?

Tarian: Yes. There is a compromise position. Suppose we admit that there *is* objective truth (thus we escape skepticism) but say that we cannot know it with certainty (thus we escape dogmatism).

Socrates: If you cannot know it with certainty, how can you know with certainty that it exists?

Tarian: You're great at sending my words back at me like a boomerang.

Socrates: Or a mirror. They are not my words, but your own.

Tarian: Let's stop talking about words and talk about real things instead.

Socrates: Gladly. For instance, is the fetus a real thing?

Tarian: Must you always come back to the fetus?

Socrates: If I serve the common master, yes; the argument always comes back to that.

Tarian: How can you be certain all arguments do? You haven't looked at all the arguments yet. You're prejudiced—you of all people! How do you know ahead of time that all my arguments are going to be weaker than yours?

Arguments do not win by strength.

Socrates: But Professor, surely as a philosopher you must know that it is not a matter of strength, as if arguments were opponents dueling. You hope to add arguments to your side and to defeat me with their weight (though we have seen none yet that stand). But yesterday's argument cannot be bypassed. It must first be answered, for if the fetus is a person, abortion is murder, and all of today's arguments fail.

Tarian: But you must answer them just as I must answer yours.

Socrates: Indeed. But I have answered yours by mine, while you have not answered mine by yours. If the fetus is a person, then it follows, for instance, that anti-abortion laws are not unduly restrictive. On the other hand, it does not follow that if laws should be as unrestrictive as possible, then a fetus is not a person.

Issue #1 is still #1.

Tarian: Frankly, Socrates, I'm getting sick of all this logic.

Socrates: Are you sure it isn't the whiskey?

Tarian: Be practical, Socrates. You just can't run a state by logic.

Socrates: By what, then? Illogic? Blind prejudice? Unexamined feelings?

Tarian: Not by philosophy, surely. This argument, for instance—it's just a war of words. It's pointless.

Socrates: No wonder your history is so full of wars. You will not fight with words, so you fight instead with guns and bombs. Have you ever tried the alternative?

Tarian: You are hopelessly utopian, Socrates.

Socrates: No, hopefully utopian. It is you who are hopeless. You have no hope in the god within us, only the animal within us.

Tarian: The god within us? You mean you worship your own reasoning?

Socrates: Not reasoning but reason. And not *my* reason but the divine reason. Have you never heard of the light that enlightens every man?

Tarian: And what do you mean by the animal within us? The body?

Socrates: Yes, and these two parts of us seem to in-

Reason as a foothold in Truth

habit two different worlds. Do not animals share with us this world of practical needs and changing circumstances? But only we humans inhabit also a world of Truth that does not change, however changeably and fitfully and fallenly we inhabit it. Reason is our foothold in that world. Do you want to withdraw your feet and even kick the dust of that world off your shoes?

Tarian: That's just what I can't buy, Socrates, that dualism of yours: two separate worlds for body and soul, real and ideal.

Socrates: Is it not you who in practice separate them more than I? You separate positive laws from moral ideals, business from goodness, politics from philosophy. "Poor Plato" indeed—to think there could be a meeting between law and morality, power and wisdom, king and philosopher, might and right.

Tarian: The State has no business trying to make people virtuous. Morality cannot be forced.

Socrates: I agree that morality cannot be forced, though perhaps it can be taught. What follows?

Tarian: That laws can't make people good.

Socrates: If laws are a matter of force rather than of teaching (which I do not admit), that follows. But even if laws can't make people good, can they not prevent people from being bad?

Tarian: No, only from *doing* bad.

Socrates: An excellent distinction, Professor, and I accept your correction. But do you not see what it entails? The doing of good or evil is in the visible, external world; being good or evil is in the soul, the character, which is invisible. So you agree with my two worlds after all.

Tarian: Let me try again. Morality is free; law compels; therefore morality is not a matter of law. Now how's that for short and sweet?

Socrates: Short, it certainly is. As for sweet, must we not taste and see before we judge?

Tarian: Taste away then. I've offered you your syllogism sandwich.

Socrates: Let us taste it, then. Morality is free, you say. Is it free from goodness as well as from evil?

Tarian: I mean it is not bound.

Socrates: Is it not bound to the service of goodness?

Tarian: You might say that.

Socrates: Indeed I might. In fact, I did. Now let us look at the other half of your sandwich. The law compels, you say?

Tarian: Yes.

Socrates: A human law can be disobeyed, can it not?

Tarian: Of course.

Socrates: So it seems as if law presupposes the freedom of choice to obey or disobey.

Tarian: That freedom, yes. Free choice.

Socrates: Just as morality does.

Tarian: Oh, Socrates, that's just another of your tricks with words. The practical fact is that you can't make people good merely by laws.

Socrates: Merely by laws? I quite agree. Laws are not *sufficient*. But that does not mean they are not *necessary*. Would not a society without laws be barbaric?

Tarian: Yes—or else saintly.

Socrates: I know of many cases of the former. Do you know of any cases of the latter?

Tarian: You have a point there. Let's get on to my third argument, if you don't mind. We've already spent far too much time on the first two.

Socrates: I don't mind. But how do you judge how

Is morality free?

Does law compel?

*Tarian's
third
objection:
unenforce-
able laws
should not
exist.*

much time is too much, if I may ask?

Tarian: You may ask, but I may not answer. Just tell me how you answer my third argument for legalizing abortion: anti-abortion laws are unenforceable.

Socrates: And therefore should not exist?

Tarian: Right.

Socrates: You understand, of course, what premise you must assume in order to make that argument work?

Tarian: Of course: unenforceable laws should not exist.

Socrates: So if we find some unenforceable law that should exist, your premise is false and your argument is defeated.

Tarian: Yes, but I challenge you to find one.

Socrates: Let us take the most unenforceable law of all.

Tarian: What is that?

Socrates: The law forbidding suicide.

Tarian: Why do you call it the most unenforceable?

Socrates: A law is enforced by threat of punishment, is it not?

Tarian: Yes.

Socrates: And we cannot punish the dead, can we?

Tarian: No.

Socrates: So laws against suicide are unenforceable.

Tarian: Right. And therefore they shouldn't exist. Where they do, they are downright silly. Everyone knows that.

Socrates: I do not know that. Let us look and see whether that is so or not.

Tarian: You never take anything for granted, do you?

Socrates: No. Please tell me this: do you think we should judge which laws deserve to exist by looking

at ideals and principles or by looking at practical consequences?

Tarian: I am a utilitarian. Do you want to argue that
hoary issue now? You're an idealist, I assume.

Socrates: Yes, but let us assume your utilitarian
premise.

Tarian: Why?

Socrates: Why, because it is your ideas we are investigating, of course. Did you think my reason for arguing was to win a contest and not to serve you by show-
ing you the meaning of your own thoughts?

Tarian: All right, mirror; show me my mind.

Socrates: Would you say that if a law would probably
lead to better consequences, it should be enacted?

Tarian: Yes.

Socrates: Now, would you say that suicide is good?

Tarian: Of course not ... well, that depends on what
you mean by *good*. I don't believe in your absolute,
universal moral values. I would not condemn all suicide as evil. It depends on the situation.

Socrates: Would you say that, all other things being
equal, it is better to have a society in which there are
fewer suicides rather than more?

Tarian: Of course.

Socrates: All right. Now—is a law the expression of
the will of the society?

Tarian: In a democracy it is, yes.

Socrates: And the social will is a sort of pressure on
the individuals in that society, is it not? Are we not
influenced—*conditioned,* I believe, is the current favorite word—by our society's expectations of us?

Tarian: Indeed we are. You seem to be coming
around more to my position, Socrates.

Socrates: I am only exploring your position, Professor. Now tell me please: if a society enacts a law against suicide, will the people be influenced by it to some extent? So that there should be fewer suicides if there is such a law than if there is not?

Tarian: It wouldn't make much difference, you know. Suicide laws have very little effect. There is such a law on the books in many countries, and still there are many suicides.

Socrates: More or fewer than if there were no such laws?

Tarian: Perhaps a bit fewer. But not many.

Socrates: If the law deterred even one suicide a century in a society of a billion people, would it not be worth the trouble to have such a law? Little is lost in making a law, but much is lost in a single suicide: a human life, and from the suicide's point of view the whole world. So an anti-suicide law is a good law by your utilitarian standards. Yet it is totally unenforceable. Therefore not all unenforceable laws are bad laws, and the premise of your third argument against anti-abortion laws topples. In fact, the argument falls a second time, for I think we can also see the falsity of its other premise, that anti-abortion laws are wholly unenforceable. Shall we explore that road now?

Tarian: That back alley, you mean, with butcher surgeons and black-market abortions and coat hangers. That's the consequence of anti-abortion laws: a lot of needless suffering and even death that could be avoided by keeping abortion safe and legal.

Socrates: Safe for whom? Certainly not for the millions of poisoned, burned, cut or suctioned fetuses who have already died where abortion is "safe and legal." It is not clear just what the consequences of

Is abortion safe for the fetus?

anti-abortion laws would be nor how well they could be enforced. But it is quite clear what the consequences of legalized abortion are: suffering and death that could be avoided by keeping the fetus safe rather than keeping abortion safe.

Tarian: You are begging the question again by treating the fetus as a person.

Socrates: And you are begging the question again by treating it as a nonperson. Once again we are back to yesterday's argument. And once again I ask you: have you any refutation of that argument?

Back to issue #1

Tarian: No, but I have two more arguments that you have not refuted yet, though I suspect they will fare about as well as two ants in the path of an elephant.

Socrates: Say rather like two clouds in the path of the sun.

Tarian: Whatever. But surely you do not disagree with my fourth point, that every child should be a wanted child?

Tarian's fourth objection: every child a wanted child

Socrates: A noble goal, indeed; but how do we attain it? By murdering the children who are unwanted or by learning to want the ones we already have?

Tarian: That's assuming a fetus is a child.

Socrates: And once again we are back in yesterday's issue.

Tarian: That was fast. You had no pity on that argument.

Socrates: Abortion is also fast, and has no pity on its victim.

Tarian: Hmmph. You have no pity on poor women who are accidentally and unwillingly pregnant. Where's your compassion? What about rape victims? Would you force a young, ignorant victim of rape to bear a child?

Objection #5: compassion

Socrates: I see we are up to your fifth argument already.

Tarian: Answer my question, please.

Socrates: Gladly, if you will answer one of mine: are any of these unwillingly pregnant women victims of murder?

Tarian: What? Of course not. How could a dead woman have a baby?

Isn't murder a worse victimization than rape?

Socrates: That would be a worse victimization, would it not? To be deprived of life is even worse than to be deprived of virginity or freedom, is it not?

Tarian: Yes . . .

Socrates: But the fetus *is* deprived of life. Where is your compassion to the fetus? Your ethic of compassion seems pretty selective; it is compassionate to one victim but not to the other.

Tarian: Hmmph. So you would force even the rape victim to bear the child.

Socrates: No, the rapist did that. I would simply forbid her to murder it, answering a grave evil with a graver one.

Tarian: Once again, you assume the fetus is a person.

Socrates: And once again, you assume it is not. What do we have left?

Tarian: Two sips of whiskey and a growing headache; that's about it.

Socrates: That hardly seems to be a buffer against the charge of advocating murder!

Tarian: ~~Socrates:~~ Socrates, I think you lack all compassion. I'll bet you weren't a wanted child yourself; you must have made life one perpetual headache for your parents. I wish your mother had been pro-choice. If you're an example of the sanctity of life, I'll take sin, thank you. Oooh! My headache is getting worse. I don't know if it's the cheap whiskey or the cheap arguments. Blast it all, Rex, why couldn't you get Chivas Regal?

Herrod: I'm afraid the dialog has degenerated into verbal abuse. Let's stop before someone's feelings are hurt, if it isn't already too late.

Tarian: It's much too late. My feelings are already hung over.

Socrates: My feelings are in no danger.

Tarian: That's because you don't have any.

Socrates: But we seem to have consumed the last of the wine.

Herrod: Perhaps we could try one more time, under more amiable circumstances—perhaps under the gentle aegis of a good facilitator?

Socrates: Is that one of your modern machines?

Herrod: No. A facilitator is a practical group psychologist. I know a wonderful one who is in Athens right now, vacationing from America.

The need for a psychologist

Socrates: A strange and fantastic land indeed. What does he do in America?

Herrod: He facilitates group encounters.

Socrates: What are group encounters? They sound like wars.

Herrod: No, no. The encounters are only verbal.

Socrates: Then by all means let us encounter him.

Tarian: It's not what you think, Socrates.

Socrates: All the better then; I shall have the joy of surprise and the advantage of acquiring some new knowledge. Where and when shall we meet again?

Herrod: In room 399 in the psychiatric ward, if you will come. Tomorrow afternoon. All right?

Socrates: All right.

Herrod: What about you, Attila?

Tarian: Oh, all right. I'm terribly dissatisfied with today.

Socrates: That's what we Athenians said after the Peloponnesian War.

Herrod: I think the reason for your disappointment was the cold and abstract and impersonal talk. My friend should help us to remember who we are: human beings.

Socrates: That is precisely my lifelong quest. If he can help us in that, I will be in his debt. All my talk today was also for that purpose: to help remind us of who we are, or who we once were—fetuses, your victims, Doctor Herrod.

Herrod: Uh... I can't handle that remark right now. I'm glad we agreed to have my friend come tomorrow; I think he will make us all more amiable. Good-bye for now.

Socrates: Good-bye.

Herrod: I wonder where he's going.

Tarian: To the heaven of absolutes where he belongs, I hope. Come on, let's get back to the real world and real philosophers where we belong: back through the door to the convention.

Herrod: Somehow it seems disappointingly conventional.

Tarian: You're beginning to sound like a certain philosopher we both know.

Herrod: Saints preserve us! It must be catching. Quick! Let's get out of this garden and back to the philosophy convention before it's too late.

Tarian: If it's not too late already.

DIALOG THREE
SOCRATES IN A PSYCHIATRIC WARD

time: *the third day*
place: *room 399 in the psychiatric ward of a hospital in Athens*

dramatis personae:
Socrates
Dr. Rex Herrod, abortionist
Professor Attila Tarian, ethicist
"Pop" Syke, psychologist

Herrod: This is Room 399, isn't it?

Tarian: Yes.

Herrod: Then it's the right place. Socrates should be here any minute. Thanks for coming with Attila and me, Pop.

Syke: I'm eager to meet this strange character. Does he really think he's Socrates?

Herrod: I think so but sometimes it's hard to tell when he's serious and when he's playful. Sometimes he seems to be both at the same time.

Syke: That is unusual. By the way, thanks for letting me hear those two tapes of your conversations.

Herrod: What do you make of him, Pop?

Syke: Of course, it's too early to tell yet. I haven't even met him. But I'm confident I can tame him.

Herrod: How can you be so sure? The last conversation ended badly.

Tarian: That was mostly my fault, I'm afraid. We philosophers tend to forget other people's feelings sometimes. That's why we asked you here, Pop.

Syke: Just what do you expect of me, if you don't mind my asking?

Herrod: Well, we suspect he has some pent-up guilt or fear or need or something. That must be why he's so rationalistic and moralistic. We hope you can help him cough up his problems with your method of "positive stroking" and "self-esteem stimulation reinforcement" and help him to be his own best friend and all those other things you do. Do you think it'll work?

Syke: I'm sure it will.

Tarian: How can you be so sure if you haven't even met him?

Syke: It's a general principle: honey attracts flies better than vinegar, as they say. It's also a matter of practice and experience. In all my years of practice, I've always found even the coldest and hardest hearts softening up when treated with the magic potion.

Tarian: What's the magic potion?

Syke: Compassion. Really, it's quite scientific, not magic. It's the principle of cause and effect. Like begets like. Compassion begets compassion just as fire begets fire. Trust someone else and they learn to trust you. It's worked for me even when everything else failed. I've done it with criminals on death row. So I have high hopes of establishing rapport with this strange little man—rap rapport, I call it. *The method of compassion*

Herrod: He'll try to steer your rap session into an argument, you know. That's his way of avoiding getting in touch with his feelings.

Syke: How do you know that? Have you psychoanalyzed him?

Herrod: You're beginning to sound like him yourself.

Syke: You make him sound like some sort of disease. I have no objection to playing word games if it helps me to be *with* him, because that will help him to be with me. I'll play anybody's game with anybody. I'll "become all things to all men so that I might by any means win some," as a great biblical psychologist put it long ago.

Tarian: St. Paul? But I thought he was full of terrible hang-ups.

Syke: Oh, he was, of course. I wish I had been around to help him. But he was a genius too. I'm good at helping geniuses.

Tarian: Well, this genius is not going to take well to your strategy: arguing with him just to soften his psyche. He thinks arguing is the way to discover truth. I think he'll feel patronized. But I don't think he'd mind. I've never seen his feelings hurt. In fact, I've never seen his feelings at all.

Syke: And that hurts *your* feelings?

Tarian: Yes, frankly. But we brought you here to work with him, not me.

Herrod: You know, I think I saw a little feeling in him.

Tarian: When?

Herrod: Toward the end of his conversation with me, when he accused me of being foolish. He seemed like a tired old schoolmaster chiding a pupil who had just repeated a mistake the master had seen over and over again for generations. He seemed sort of impatiently patient with me.

Syke: And how did that make you feel?

Herrod: As Attila said, you're here for him, not for us, if you don't mind.

Syke: Please don't feel threatened.

Herrod: I'm not feeling threatened, damn you!

Tarian: I hope your honey works better on Socrates than it's doing on Rex, Pop.

Syke: Patience, my friends. The gentle approach takes time, but the force of compassion is an irresistible force, I assure you.

Herrod: And Socrates is an immovable object. So what happens when an irresistible force meets an immovable object?

Tarian: Perhaps we're about to see. But I wonder whether there can be both an irresistible force and an immovable object in the same universe. That seems to be a contradiction.

Syke: I thought you didn't believe reasoning could discover real truth about the universe.

Tarian: Are you playing Socrates now, until he comes?

Syke: If I were, I'd conclude that logically either Socrates will be moved or I will be resisted.

Tarian: He's not even here and already you've caught the infection!

Socrates (entering): What am I, then? A communicable disease?

Tarian: Oh, Socrates! I didn't see you come in. I was only kidding, you know, as you were yesterday at the philosophy convention.

Socrates: Was I?

Tarian: How should I know? I'm only a philosopher, not a psychologist. Speaking of psychologists, why don't you meet my friend, Pop Syke?

Socrates: Why don't I? But I do. Hello, Dr. Syke.

Syke: Hello, Socrates. Please call me "Pop." I'm very glad to meet you.

Socrates: Why?

Syke: What?

Socrates: Why? Why are you very glad to meet me?

Syke: Oh, because Rex and Attila here have told me so much about you, and they played for me your last two days' conversations on tape.

Socrates: Ah, yes. Your external mind.

Syke: What?

Socrates: No matter. What is the plan for today?

Syke: Rex and Attila want to just sit and listen this time while we talk, if that's all right with you. And do you mind if we tape this conversation too?

Socrates: Of course not. But is the conversation to be about the same issue?

Syke: What issue?

Socrates: Why, what we were discussing the last two

days: the morality of abortion.

Syke: I'm interested in *you*, Socrates.

Socrates: So far we share no common interest. I look
.for a map and you offer me a mirror.

Syke: What? I'm surprised at you, Socrates. Aren't
you forgetting your life's task, "know thyself"?

Socrates: Oh, but surely that does not mean to know
the ins and outs of my particular body or soul, but to
know my nature, which is universal. What is it to be
human? That is my great question.

Syke: But I'm interested in you not just as a specimen
of the species but as an individual—as a friend, in
fact. Please don't think I think of you as an object.

Socrates: I would not consider that an insult, as you
seem to. I often think of myself as an object.

Syke: And I suppose you classify yourself among
other objects?

Socrates: Of course. Genus, animal. Difference, rational. Species, rational animal. Alternatively, a soul
using a body. Don't you ever think about yourself in
this way?

Syke: No. I'd rather be your friend than to know your
definition.

Socrates: But how can you be truly a friend to someone whose essence you do not know?

Syke: I don't want to argue with you. I just want to
be friends with you.

Socrates: Why?

Syke: What?

Socrates: That's the second time you seemed surprised at the question *Why?* Surely it is a simple one,
a child's question, in fact.

Syke: I'm surprised you ask for reasons for my wanting to be your friend.

Socrates: The choice is a free one, is it not?

Syke: Yes.

Socrates: And presumably you have some reasons for the free choices you make?

Syke: Can't we just be friends without arguing?

Socrates: Let's see whether we can or not. A friend is someone who helps you, is it not?

Syke: Oh, boy. Here we go. All right, yes.

Socrates: And you would help me if you made me happy, would you not?

Syke: Yes indeed.

Socrates: Very well, then. It is finding the truth that makes me happy. And it is argument that enables me to find the truth. So if you are truly my friend, you will help me by arguing with me. For I find that in this great quest two travel much faster than one, and the truth emerges like sparks from struck flint and steel when two minds come together in dialog. Will you be flint for me and strike against my steel? It would be to your advantage also.

Friendship and argument

Syke: Why? Do you have some truth in your pocket for me?

Socrates: I do not believe that any teacher ever puts truth into another's mind, but only helps the other's mind to teach itself, to dis-cover or un-cover the truth lying hidden within. I know of three arts like that: teaching, farming and medicine. Each merely brings out the inner life and health of its object rather than changing it from without. The mind teaches itself when aided with apt questions; a farmer does not grow food, but it grows itself under his care; and a doctor does not heal, but the body heals itself under his treatment. Now we seem to have a fourth art which falls under this principle: the healing of the psyche.

Teaching, farming, medicine and practical psychology as unique arts

Syke: You see, Socrates, I am very much like you. Your Socratic method does not force truth on a person. And I do not force anyone to change. I am pro-freedom, pro-choice.

Socrates: Are you also pro-choice concerning abortion?

Syke: Yes. Must we talk about that instead of about ourselves?

Socrates: Only if you will be my friend. I too am pro-choice, though not concerning abortion. I will not force my will on you, or on a fetus. Will you be my friend and argue with me about this matter?

Syke: I'd really rather talk about us than about this other matter. Why is it so important to you?

Socrates: Everything is important to me. But especially a matter of life and death, which is what abortion surely is.

Syke: All right, go ahead. Talk about abortion.

Socrates: I would rather hear you talk about it. Why are you for it?

Syke: I'm not for abortion. I'm for choice. I'm pro-choice.

Socrates: Why?

Syke: Why am I for choice? Because I'm against the use of force. I like everyone just the way they are.

Is abortion pro-choice or pro-force? *Socrates:* Isn't abortion the use of force? Isn't it a forceful change for the fetus to change from living to dead? You say you like everyone just the way they are; but the abortionist certainly does not like the fetus just the way it is, alive.

Syke: That sounds like a very harsh saying to me, Socrates.

Socrates: Abortion is a harsh reality, is it not? Should our speaking not reflect things as they are?

Syke: I feel quite put out when you say that, Socrates. You sound uncomfortably judgmental to me.

Socrates: And you'd like me to change? Because you like me just the way I am?

Syke: That sounds like a logical contradiction, I know. But logical contradictions don't bother me, as they bother you.

Socrates: Then for your own sake I hope *you* change. Do you want me to help you, as a friend?

Syke: If you'll accept my help only on the condition of a give-and-take, that's fine. Perhaps we can help each other. But my thing is feeling, not thinking. No, wait, Socrates, that's not as blind and irrational as it sounds to you. One thing—one very, very important thing—you always seem to forget: words express feelings as much as they express thoughts. In fact, feelings are prior because thoughts are usually motivated by feelings, not vice versa. Reasons are usually rationalizations—rationalizations of prior feelings. Now I'd like to help you get in touch with your feelings, perhaps for the first time in your life. Ordinarily I charge $75 for forty-five minutes, but for you I'll be here as long as you need me and for free. How does that sound? How does that make you feel?

Are reasons rationalizations of feelings?

Socrates: If it's a confession of feelings you want, I can offer you one quite easily. My first feeling, when I heard you say that logical contradictions don't bother you, was pity. I felt as if I were watching a carpenter who deliberately blunted his cutting tools. Second, when you said I was judgmental to speak of abortion as I did, I felt disappointment that you had forgotten the distinction between judging the sin and judging the sinner that I made yesterday, and the excuse I offered for women seeking abortions, that an abor-

Socrates' feelings

tionist society and philosophy had filched them of both reason and instinct. Third, when you said you believed that most reasons were rationalizations, I felt a little relief that you didn't say what I had feared you would say, that *all* reasoning is rationalization. At least, I thought, you are not such a fool as to directly contradict yourself, for if all reasoning is only rationalization, so is that piece of reasoning. Fourth, when you offered me your free service of feeling-touching, I felt puzzlement. I wondered why so many people would pay so much money to explore the coverings of thought. For feelings, it seems to me, usually cover and obscure thought. But I suspect there is a good answer to this question somewhere, and that it is a defect in myself not to see it. Fifth, I still feel puzzled why you think feelings are more important than thought, for we share feelings with the higher animals, while rational thought raises us above them. But this, I suppose, is more a thought than a feeling. Those are all the feelings I can remember, at any rate, in the last few minutes. Is that the sort of thing you wanted?

Syke: Socrates, I see we have a very formidable series of blocks to deal with here.

Socrates: Blocks? But I have freely confessed to you all the feelings and all the thoughts I had since I met you. I assure you, I held nothing back for fear of hurting your feelings.

Syke: Oh, I believe that, all right, Socrates. You told me all your conscious thoughts and feelings. But we have to do some digging to get at your subconscious ones, you know.

Socrates: And you want to do that now, rather than respond to any of the many thoughts I just expressed to you?

Syke: Yes. That is my vocation.

Socrates: Well, dig away, then. Perhaps it will bring a little light and not just darkness. I am committed to seek the knowledge of all things human and divine. That is my vocation. What feelings do you want to dig up?

Syke: I want to find out how you really feel toward a woman who has had an abortion.

Socrates: I have told you already, if you had ears to hear. Has your external mind failed you already?

Syke: What do you mean?

Socrates: Do you not remember what I said on the tapes? That's the problem with an external thing: it still needs to be internalized. The memory of a tape memory cannot itself be a tape.

Syke: Would you refresh my bad memory, then?

Socrates: Gladly. I implied yesterday and said again today that I make no judgment of personal guilt, and I say that the real murderer of these innocent millions in the womb is society's false philosophy. That is why I think it so important to cross-examine the philosophy. The fetus is the final victim, and the mother and her abortionist are victims of the philosophy. So I want to attack the first link in the chain. For I also believe this: that all evildoing is rooted in false ideas, in ignorance of the truth. This is where I begin.

Syke: I think you begin wrongly. You do not begin with compassion, but with guilt. Then you look to see where the blame should be assigned. Because you have some compassion, you choose not to place primary blame on the people involved, but on the ideas. But you begin with your sense of blame. Suppose you didn't have this big bag of guilt and blame in the first place. Then you wouldn't have to unload it on any-

How Socrates feels toward a woman who has an abortion

Blaming the philosophy first, not the person

Why any blame at all?

body or anything. Wouldn't that be a great relief? Are you sure you're not feeling guilty yourself about something? Or even about nothing, just a vague feeling of guilt? That's usually the root cause of someone pointing the finger of blame, you know.

Socrates: So you deduce from my judgment of guilt on others, even on other ideas, that I must feel guilty myself?

Syke: Subconsciously, yes.

Socrates: Do you think it is good teachers or poor teachers who can best judge who is a good teacher and who is a poor one?

Syke: Good teachers, of course, but what does that have to do with what we're talking about?

Socrates: You shall see. And is it a sick physician or one who is well who can best cure an illness in a patient?

Syke: One who is well, I suppose.

Socrates: And what about a physician of the soul? Is it the one who is healthy of soul or the one who is ill of soul who can best judge the health or illness of another soul?

Syke: If you put it in those terms, the healthy of soul can best judge.

Socrates: I do put it in those terms. And is not guilt an illness of soul, and innocence health?

Syke: Guilt is an illness, all right.

Socrates: Then it is the innocent who can best judge the guilt or innocence of another, and not the guilty. Why then do you conclude from my judgment of guilt that I must be guilty myself?

Syke: Wait a minute, there, great logician. Are you saying that your judgment of guilt proves you are innocent? There's a fallacy there somewhere.

Socrates: No, I am saying that it does not prove I am guilty, as you claim. Shall I explain to you the logic involved?

Syke: No, I think it would be *too* involved. Please, let's not play that game anymore.

Socrates: It is no game, Pop, but inquiry into how we should live. Can you think of a more serious business than that?

Syke: Anything you say, Socrates.

Socrates: No, no. It is not I who say we must inquire, but the common master.

Syke: Yes, I am quite familiar with your personification of your own thinking processes. Please don't be insulted, but friends are honest with each other, and I feel this is unworthy of you, my friend. I should think you would have stopped talking to imaginary friends when you stopped being a child.

Is reason objective or subjective?

Socrates: The common master is no more mine than the light of the sun, and no more imaginary. If you do not accept his light, we cannot talk together, you and I, but only grope apart and feel around in each other's darkness. Is this what your work consists of?

Syke: Oh, Socrates, let's at least be friends. Let's be together, whether in the light or in the darkness.

Socrates: But do not friends share all things in common? Yet you will not share the light in which I live.

Syke: You mean the light of reason?

Socrates: Yes. Will you explore the common light with me for a while? Then, if you insist, we can try to explore the individual darkness that you call the subconscious.

Syke: All right. That's only fair. Now, where were we?

Socrates: I was refuting your argument that I must

have a great load of guilt because I judged about the guilt of abortion.

Syke: Oh, yes. Well, I'm sorry if I hurt your feelings.

Socrates: You didn't hurt my feelings. You hurt your own thinking.

Syke: What do you mean?

Socrates: You contradicted yourself.

Syke: How?

Should we judge those who judge?

Socrates: Judging me for being judgmental is being judgmental yourself, is it not? Either it is right to judge, or not. If so, it is right for me to judge. If not, it is wrong for you to judge me. Worse, in fact, for I only judged the act, but you judged the person.

Syke: That's a clever argument, Socrates.

Socrates: I'm not interested in compliments, or in cleverness, but in truth. Is the conclusion of the argument proved to be true, or not?

Syke: Socrates, I must be honest with you. I'm getting impatient with all this logic. I'm just not interested in arguments, only in helping you.

Socrates: But you can best help me by helping me see the truth by refuting my argument, if it is wrong.

Syke: No, I think I can better help you by helping you to unload your inner garbage truck. Just let go all the guilt you feel. It's garbage. Flush it down the psychic toilet.

Socrates: You wish to remove the sense of guilt from everyone?

Syke: To help them remove it from themselves, yes.

Socrates: Even from the most wicked?

Is guilt a source of evil?

Syke: Yes! You see, it was the terrible sense of guilt and self-hatred that made them do wicked things in the first place. Bad feelings are the source of bad deeds. If you feel good about yourself, you feel good about others too, and then you do good to them. If you feel bad about yourself, you feel bad about others too, and you do bad to them. People who feel good don't make trouble.

Socrates: Oh, but doesn't a great and wicked tyrant feel good as long as he is successful? Doesn't a sadist find cruelty positively delightful? Don't we all enjoy lording it over others now and then? Is it not the absence of guilt that allows many people to commit their crimes? And is it not the function of guilt to prevent wrongdoing or, after it is done, to prevent its repetition? So it would appear that the effect of your work is to remove this barrier to evil, to abolish conscience and to allow us to enjoy the pleasures of sin without the anguish of remorse.

Or a barrier to evil?

Syke: Wow! That's quite an indictment. You're all for guilt, are you?

Socrates: When it is a true insight into deed and character, yes; when it is a false feeling with no true object, no. When it works to prevent crime, yes; when it works to produce irrational self-hatred, no.

Syke: I don't find those distinctions to work in practice. Guilt is guilt. It feels the same no matter how you rationalize it.

Socrates: Will you not even make the distinction between the sin and the sinner?

The distinction between sinner and sin

Syke: That's a medieval distinction. Straight from the Inquisition.

Socrates: On the contrary, I suspect that it was precisely the refusal to make that distinction that helped cause the Inquisition. They too failed to distinguish the sinner and the sin, so they hated and tortured both.

Syke: And I'm compassionate to both.

Socrates: To both? Is it compassion to the patient to be compassionate to the disease?

Syke: False analogy, Socrates. Disease is real. Sin is a superstition.

Socrates: Suppose I deliberately give you a terrible disease. The disease is real. The act of mine is also real. Now is this a good act or an evil act?

Syke: An evil act, of course.

Is evil real?

Socrates: Really? I mean, is the evil of the act real? Or is it just a superstition?

Syke: Oh, Socrates, you're just hung up on your good-or-evil characterizations. For you everything has to fit into those two moralistic little boxes.

Socrates: I'm not asking about everything now, just about the act of giving you a terrible disease. You admitted that this act fit into the category of evil, did you not?

Syke: I'm not going to crawl into your little boxes with you, Socrates. You keep harping on good and evil. When will you come out of your fairy tale into the real world? Life is for real, man.

Socrates: I'm not sure what that means, and I suspect it would be pointless to try to find out. As for fairy tales, I find life very much like them.

Syke: You mean you find them like life?

Is life like a fairy tale?

Socrates: No, I find life like them. You see, they are for you what myths were for us. Realistic stories are like life, but myths and fairy tales are larger than life. Life is like them.

Syke: So life is like a fairy tale, is it?

Socrates: Yes.

Syke: I suppose you brought along a magic wand?

Socrates: As a matter of fact, I did. Would you like to see me use it?

Syke: Yes. What magic can you do?

Socrates: How about anti-gravity? I can make a heavy object rise into the air by the force of my will and the touch of my wand.

Syke: I don't think that's a very funny joke at all, Socrates.

Socrates: It's not a joke. I mean it.

Syke: All right, then; move this building for me with your magic.

Socrates: Unfortunately, my magic is not quite that strong. But I could make that heavy book over there on the table rise into the air with my magic wand.

Syke: Go ahead.

Socrates: All right. (Picks up the book with his hand.)

Syke: Very cute.

Socrates: Yes, it is. I'm glad to see that your wonder is not dulled by familiarity, as it is in most adults.

Syke: All right, you win one. Life is wonderful. But now let's get back from fairy tales to plain talk.

Socrates: Ah, but the fairy tales are full of very plain talk, especially about good and evil. That's one of the things that makes them so realistic. But we should be focusing on our issue, shouldn't we? Not just good and evil in general but whether abortion is good or evil. Have you anything to add to our argument?

Syke: I think I do. Your argument dealt almost en- tirely with the fetus. I think it's time to put in a word for the mothers.

Socrates: Let us consider the mothers, by all means. What word do you want to put in for them?

Syke: That they have rights.

Socrates: I agree. Now let us see where we disagree. Why do you say they have rights? Is it because they are persons?

Syke: I guess so.

Socrates: Let's see whether we can take it beyond a guess to knowing. Do stones have rights?

Syke: No.

Socrates: Do plants?

Syke: No. People do.

Socrates: Simply because they are people?

Syke: Yes

Socrates: So if a fetus is a person, it too has rights. As

"*A person's a person no matter how small.*" it is written in the great classic of your literature, *Horton Hears a Who:* "A person's a person, no matter how small."

Syke: But a fetus is not a person.

Socrates: So we are back to our original argument again, just as we kept being led back to it yesterday. Have you anything to say about that?

Syke: No. I want to talk about women's rights.

Socrates: All right. What do you mean by *women's rights?*

Women's rights *Syke:* Well, I believe a woman should have reproductive freedom. The right not to bear a child if she doesn't want to. The right to do as she pleases with her own body. The right not to be a slave of nature, a baby-making machine. The right to dignity, the dignity of women—people, not machines. Furthermore . . .

Socrates: Excuse me, please, but could you do me a great favor?

Syke: What?

Socrates: Friends accommodate to each other, and you said you wanted to be a friend to me, so would you accommodate my slow mind by helping me sort out all these things you've said already before you go on with more?

Syke: What all did I say?

Socrates: Five things, if I'm not mistaken.

Syke: Did I, really?

Socrates: Well, let's see. You said that women should have, first, "reproductive freedom," whatever that is. Perhaps it is to be identified with the second thing, the right not to bear a child. Third, there is a right to do whatever she pleases with her body; fourth, a right not to be a slave of nature, which you identified with being "a baby-making machine"; and fifth, the right to the dignity of women as people, not machines. Have I got that right?

Syke: Socrates, that's positively pathological.

Socrates: Oh, I don't think it's as bad as all that. A bit vague and fuzzy around the edges, perhaps, but we may be able to get one or two meaningful statements out of it if we try.

Syke: You're toying with me. I didn't mean my speech; I meant yours.

Socrates: But my speech was only a mirror of yours. What in mine elicited that term of supreme pity and contempt from a psychologist, *pathological*?

Syke: You cut my speech into five neat little pieces like a mother cutting a piece of meat for a baby.

Socrates: The statements were yours, not mine. All I did was to count them. Is it pathological to count up to five?

Syke: You know, you're really fascinating, Socrates. I've never met anyone like you before.

Socrates: That is indeed a great defect in your educational experience. I trust we can remedy it.

Syke: How? What are you going to do now?

Socrates: It's what *you* are going to do, Pop. You are going to give an account of what you say.

Syke: What do you mean?

Socrates: Precisely my question. Have you never played the game, as you call it, of explaining and defending what you say with reason?

Syke: Not your way.

Socrates: But this is not *my* way, Pop. This is no contest of persons or wills, but of ideas. I'm sorry to seem so tedious, but since you keep referring to the laws of the common master as if they were my own private property, I must correct you and defend them. It is not *The* my way that is the master, but *the* way, the *logos*. And *common* serving this master is no game. It is my life's purpose.

The common master

Syke: I hear you, Socrates.

Socrates: You hear me with your ears, but do you hear me with your mind?

Syke: I hear you with my heart.

Socrates: I wonder whether your heart has eyes. Do you understand?

Syke: Yes, that's what I meant.

Socrates: Then you agree.

Syke: No.

Socrates: Then you don't understand, because if you did, I think you would have to agree.

Syke: I just don't see reason as any kind of god.

Socrates: I'd rather put it the other way round: I see God as utterly reasonable. But let us proceed anyway. I see you would rather shine your little flashlight on the issue than expose it to the light of the sun. Very well, let us examine your words about the rights of women. First of all, what do you mean by *reproductive freedom*?

Are women slaves of nature?

Syke: I want women to be free, not slaves of nature.

Socrates: So you said. But what do you mean by it? Do you mean you want them to be free from their own nature? How can that be? How can a thing be free from its own nature and still be itself?

Syke: I just want them to be free to be whatever they want to be.

Socrates: Birds, for instance?

Syke: That's ridiculous, Socrates.

Socrates: My point exactly.

Syke: I guess you want a better definition.

Socrates: You are a good guesser.

Syke: Well, then, I guess I mean by reproductive freedom simply the freedom not to have children if she doesn't want to. That's clear and simple, isn't it?

Socrates: We cannot be sure until we look. A woman has a child by getting pregnant, correct?

Syke: Yes.

Socrates: And she gets pregnant by sexual intercourse, correct?

Syke: Of course.

Socrates: And sexual intercourse is either forced, in the case of rape, or voluntary, correct?

Syke: Yes.

Socrates: And the forced is unfree and the voluntary free?

Syke: Yes.

Socrates: Then except for victims of rape, women *do* have what you call reproductive freedom.

Who has reproductive freedom?

Syke: Socrates! What a simple-minded slap in the face!

Socrates: Perhaps I am simple-minded, but how is this a slap in the face?

Syke: Women are crying out for reproductive freedom, and your response is: "If you don't like the heat, get out of the kitchen." If you don't want kids, don't have intercourse.

Socrates: That seems to me to be a reasonable saying. Kitchens naturally generate heat, unless equipped with cooling devices, and intercourse naturally generates babies, unless equipped with contraceptive devices.

Syke: I suppose you're against contraception too?

Socrates: Not until I examine it, surely. One thing at a time, please. We are discussing abortion today (and not making much progress, I fear). The statement of mine that seemed offensive to you was that women already have what you call reproductive freedom unless they are raped. They can freely choose among *Five* five alternatives: chastity, contraception, abortion, *alternatives:* adoption, or motherhood. All I say is that the third *chastity,* alternative, abortion, is evil, and that one of the other *contraception,* four is always available and always preferable. *abortion,*

adoption, *Syke:* Always preferable? But it may involve great *motherhood* suffering. Why is it always preferable?

Socrates: Because it is always preferable to suffer evil rather than to commit it.

Syke: First a slap, then a sermon! I'd give them compassion instead—something I've seen none of in you.

Socrates: This thing you keep speaking of—compassion—is it a virtue?

Syke: Of course.

Socrates: Then I would be grateful to you for helping me to acquire it, for I think there is nothing nobler or more necessary than a complete stock of virtues.

Syke: Well, now, perhaps we're getting somewhere. I think I may be able to help you there, Socrates.

Socrates: Then would you help me take the first step toward the acquiring of this precious thing?

Syke: What's that?

Socrates: Why, telling me what it is, of course, so

that when I find it I may recognize it and clasp it to myself and not let it go because I confuse it with some other, less precious thing.

Syke: You mean you want a *definition* of compassion?

Socrates: How else am I to recognize it?

Syke: Must you always be so theoretical?

Socrates: I am being most practical. It is for the sake of actually gaining a virtue that I seek to know what a virtue is, so that I can avoid the very practical danger of confusing it with what it isn't and resting content with a mistake. So would you now help me by defining this precious virtue which you say I lack?

Syke: I don't know, Socrates. I think you just have to feel it. How can you define a feeling?

Socrates: You have just taken the first step; you gave its genus. Compassion is a feeling. Now all we need is the second half of the definition, the specific difference between this feeling and all other feelings, and we have done what we set out to do. I am surprised, though, that you think of compassion as a *virtue* if it is a feeling.

Syke: Why?

Socrates: We are praised or blamed for having or lacking a virtue, are we not?

Syke: Yes.

Socrates: And when we are praised or blamed for something, that implies that we are responsible for that thing, does it not?

Syke: Yes.

Socrates: Are we responsible for what is under our control or for what is not?

Syke: What is under our control.

Socrates: Are our deliberate choices under our control?

*A definition
of compassion*

*Compassion's
genus:
feeling*

Syke: Yes.

Socrates: Are our feelings under our control?

Syke: What do you mean?

Socrates: Can we by a rational choice "turn on" or "turn off" a feeling at will?

Syke: Of course not. Though a rationalistic fool may try.

Proof that compassion is not a virtue

Socrates: Then it follows that compassion is not a virtue.

Syke: What?

Socrates: Shall we go through the steps of the argument again?

Syke: No. Please. I'm getting sick of your "it follows that..." routine.

Socrates: That is indeed a significant fact about your psyche, but it has no significance for the validity of the argument, you know. Nor for the real truth of things.

Syke: Compassion *must* be a virtue. Everyone knows that.

Socrates: Then we must have made a mistake in our argument. If everyone is right, then we are wrong. Where did we go wrong, do you think?

Syke: Frankly, I don't care. I don't even care whether compassion is a virtue or not. The bottom line is simply that whatever compassion is, you need it.

Socrates: But the only way you can help me to acquire it is by completing the definition. We're half done; could you give me the other half of the treasure you are withholding from me?

Syke: What do you mean?

Socrates: We found the genus of compassion, feeling. Now what is its specific difference? How does it differ from other feelings?

Syke: It feels for suffering. It wants to avoid suffering in the other person.

Socrates: I see. It seems we have what we sought.

Syke: Are you satisfied now?

Socrates: With the definition, yes. With your ranking of compassion so high, no.

Syke: Why?

Socrates: Is it not those we care little about that we have only compassion for? We have compassion on strangers and acquaintances, but we care more deeply about our children. A parent causes more trouble to a child than a grandparent does; why? Because the parent loves more. If a stranger told you he was about to commit suicide, would you try as hard to stop him as you would if the person were your wife?

Syke: That's true...

Socrates: A lover cares more about your life, your virtue, even your looks, than a nonlover does.

Syke: All right, how does this connect with abortion?

Socrates: Mere compassion would be suspicious of birth itself, for birth is the door to suffering. But love would open the door.

Syke: The door to suffering?

Socrates: Yes. What life is without it? It begins in suffering; it grows through suffering; it ends in suffering. And yet it wills to live.

Syke: It?

Socrates: Excuse me. I was waxing mystical. *Babies* struggle to live. Do you know how desperately they struggle to escape the instruments of abortion?

Syke: Spare me the gory details.

Socrates: In other words, please have compassion.

Syke: Well, yes.

Socrates: Is not truth more important than com-

Compassion's specific difference: avoiding suffering

Mere compassion suspicious of birth, the door to suffering

passion?

Syke: No, not to me it isn't.

Socrates: Then I pity you. In other words, I have compassion for you.

Syke: I am simply astonished to hear you speak like this, Socrates.

Socrates: As I said before, that may be an interesting expression of your psyche, but it does not affect the facts of the matter.

A woman's right over her body

Syke: The facts of the matter are that women have legal rights over their own bodies. Whether it is compassionate or not and whether compassion is a virtue or not, abortion is a right.

Socrates: A legal right in many countries, yes. A moral right? That is another question, unless you wish to identify the two and call a tyrant's legal henchman right.

Syke: A woman has a right over her body.

Socrates: And a fetus is only a part of a woman's body, therefore she has a right over the fetus?

Syke: Exactly.

Socrates: So the argument depends on the premise that the fetus is not a person but part of the mother.

Syke: Yes.

Back to the first argument: is the fetus a person?

Socrates: And so we are back once again to our first day's argument. If a fetus is a person, abortion is murder; if not, not. And if the fetus is a person, it is not part of the mother's body, since persons are not parts of other persons. So she does not have rights over it, not the right of life and death, at any rate.

Syke: You went through that argument the first day with Rex.

Socrates: I know. Do you have any new facts or arguments to refute the conclusion of that argument?

Syke: No.

Socrates: Then let us proceed to examine your next statement, if you will. You want to liberate women from slavery to nature, which you identify with being a baby-making machine. Is that right?

Syke: That's what I said, yes.

Socrates: Now let us find out what you mean.

Syke: I mean just that a woman has a right to be free from pregnancy if she wants to be. She should not be forced to have a baby.

Socrates: Tell me, who gives her the right to be free from this slavery to nature? Is it nature that gives this right? Is it a natural right?

Can a woman be freed from nature?

Syke: You won't trap me in that contradiction, Socrates. How could nature give her the right to be free from nature?

Socrates: Is it society then?

Syke: I guess so. What else could it be?

Socrates: Perhaps some other day we could discuss some interesting alternative answers to that question. But for now let us assume that it is society that gives a woman the right to be free from nature and from pregnancy. Is it not also society that makes a woman pregnant?

Syke: What do you mean?

Socrates: Nature gave them wombs, but men fertilize them. Nature creates the potentiality, but male society actualizes it.

Syke: Of course.

Socrates: Then we had better say to the men too: "If you can't stand the heat, get out of the kitchen." That is, if you won't accept responsibility and care for your child, get out of the woman's body (which is indeed by nature a baby-making body, though not a baby-making machine). I leave aside for the moment the alternative of contraception. My point is simply that since a man is half responsible for voluntary intercourse and wholly responsible for rape, justice would seem to demand that men, not just women, find alternatives to abortion. They are the "society" that gives or refuses a woman the "right" to be free from pregnancy. And in the case of rape, it would seem just to make the rapist accept full responsibility for the child he fathered, including at least adequate finances, until the child becomes an adult. I wonder why your society has not considered such a just law instead of the more convenient injustice of abortion. Perhaps it is because the men make most of the laws? Statistics show, you know, that men consistently favor abortion more than women do.

Syke: Now you sound as uncompassionate to the men as you did to the women.

Socrates: At least it's even-handed justice—something you say nature has not given to women, since you accused nature of enslaving them by giving them wombs.

Syke: Well, doesn't it seem unfair to you that a woman bears the burden of pregnancy, literally? That a woman is born into the world with a little prison cell attached to her body?

Socrates: The inhabitant of that cell is not the mother but the fetus, and birth liberates the prisoner. Your solution to the unwanted prisoner is capital punishment, without trial or conviction of crime.

Syke: The mother is the prisoner, if she doesn't want to be pregnant. And contraception and abortion are keys to unlock her prison cell.

Socrates: You know, I believe that on a very deep

level you are a chauvinist.

Syke: What? I want to liberate women; you're the one who wants to enslave them. Where do you get off calling me a chauvinist?

Socrates: For millenia men have envied women their power to procreate and enshrined their awe in many myths of Mother Earth. Now you call this power a prison. What a blasphemy against the sacred shrine of life!

Syke: I thought you were all for justice, Socrates. Justice demands equality.

Socrates: Is it just to treat a pig like a stone, or a stone like a pig?

Syke: No.

Socrates: You see? Justice is not simple equality, but equal treatment of the equal and unequal treatment of the unequal.

Syke: So you think women are unequal to men?

Socrates: Certainly. And men unequal to women, equally so. I think women are definitely superior to men at being women, and men definitely superior to women at being men. Surely if there is any difference that is natural it is the difference between the sexes.

Syke: Not according to modern thinking, Socrates. You are hopelessly out of date and sexist. We have discovered that sexuality is societal.

Socrates: Have you, now? What new observations or experiments or arguments have revealed this astonishing new discovery, may I ask?

Syke: I could equally well ask you what proves your old sexist prejudice.

Socrates: May I distinguish two meanings of the term? If you mean by *sexism* innate sexuality, I am a sexist, just as the whole human race has been until your remarkable new discovery that sexuality is societal. But if you mean by *sexism* chauvinism, the view that women are inferior, I deny the charge. Surely not all differences are differences of inferiority and superiority. Are dogs inferior to cats, or cats to dogs?

Syke: No.

Socrates: Is their difference societal or natural?

Syke: Natural.

Socrates: Then not all natural differences are differences in value.

Syke: But in practice segregation has always meant enslavement; differences have always turned out to be discriminations.

Socrates: That is due in practice to the same cause as your mistake in thought: the confusion of justice with equality, so that the denial of equality becomes a denial of justice.

Syke: I don't understand your diagnosis, Doctor Socrates.

Chauvinists and unisexists share the same error.

Socrates: The chauvinists among you, ancient or modern, deduce from the true premise that sexual differences are innate and natural, the false conclusion that women are the inferior sex; and the unisexists among you deduce from the true premise that women are not the inferior sex the false conclusion that sexual differences are not natural. You see, both sides, far apart as they seem to be, commit the same error: they assume the false premise that all natural differences are differences in value, differences between the inferior and the superior. Deny this common premise and both arguments fall. My diagnosis is that your chauvinism and your unisexism, while seemingly opposite, are deeply similar. They both share your modern confusion between justice and equality. That's why you want to turn women into men by "liberating" them from their wombs, from their own nature, their glory and their uniqueness. That's why I called you a chauvinist. The worst kind, I think; for at least the chauvinists of the past, who spoke of women as the weaker sex, did not want to take a woman's very womanhood from her. They spoke from suppressed envy; you speak from scorn. You say you like everyone just the way they are? Apparently that does not apply to half the human race. You accuse nature of injustice. But beware. It is not a good idea to bring Mother Nature into court. It might turn out that she is the judge.

Syke: My, my! What an indictment! So you think nature always has the last word?

Socrates: Indeed I do.

Syke: That's not what you taught twenty-four centuries ago. You said the body was a prison for the soul.

Socrates: I have learned a lot since then. But even then I said *all* bodies were prisons, not just women's.

Syke: What have you learned since then that made you change your mind?

Socrates: I mistakenly thought of body and soul as enemies by nature rather than by fault. You see, I assumed that the human condition as we observe it is our natural condition, rather than an abnormal and unnatural one which may not have always been so and will not always be so. I was right, I think, to say that the existing relationship between body and soul often resembles that between prison and prisoner, but I found out after death that it need not always be so. Meanwhile, many of your modern philosophers and psychologists corrected my error from quite an-

What Socrates has learned about body and soul

other source: their experience *before* death, even in our unnatural state, of the person as a "psychosomatic unity," as they call it. Body and soul are not insulated compartments, as I thought, but whatever is innate to one always innately affects the other. You agree with this principle of psychology, do you not?

Syke: Certainly. I'm glad to see you have made some progress, Socrates.

Socrates: And do you also agree that sexuality is *biologically* innate rather than societal? Society did not *invent* sex, surely?

Syke: So?

A proof that souls are innately sexual

Socrates: So from these two premises you must come to the conclusion that souls are innately sexual.

Syke: What? Sexual *souls*? Spiritual sex? You're kidding, aren't you?

Socrates: Not at all. The argument is quite serious. How do you avoid the conclusion? Which of the two premises do you deny?

Syke: I don't know, but I do know that the conclusion just can't be true.

Socrates: How do you know that?

Syke: I don't know. I never thought about that. I just do.

Socrates: I see you are in need of my services.

Syke: Socrates, the conclusion is outrageous. You're teaching sexual stereotyping.

Socrates: And so is nature. Remember, it's not a good idea to disagree with nature. But perhaps you would be less offended if I explained that it does not seem to be monosexual stereotyping, but as one of your bright Jung men taught, *anima* and *animus*, feminine and masculine in the same soul, though with one in a priority role. For that matter, even bodies are somewhat bisexual: we have a little of each sex's hormones.

Syke: It's still stereotyping. A far cry from what you said in the *Republic* about sex.

Socrates: Oh, that wasn't me. That was purely Plato's invention. I'm surprised you charge me with all his crackpot ideas.

Syke: What crackpot ideas?

Socrates: "The only difference between them is that the female bears and the male mounts." Indeed! What nonsense!

Syke: Minimizing innate sexual differences was a very progressive idea for his time, you know.

Socrates: Regressive, I should say. Plato always did let mathematics go too much to his head, I think. By the way, he also taught in the same passage that women were inferior in every way to men. Now there's progressivism for you, right? In other words, the sexes are equal, but one is more equal than the other. That was a piece of Newthink worthy of Orwell.

Syke: You seem pretty knowledgeable in our literature.

Socrates: I have devoured libraries. But I have not tried to devour life, or sex, its fount.

Syke: And you think I do?

Socrates: Yes. You trivialize the sacred.

Syke: So you invoke the sanctity of life, eh?

Socrates: With reverence.

Syke: I must confess to you, Socrates, that I feel very suspicious when I hear anyone use that cliché.

Socrates: A truth becomes a cliché when it loses its life and only the words remain. Tell me, please, are you suspicious of sanctity or suspicious of life? These seem to me to be the two greatest things in the world,

Sexual stereotyping

All sexes are equal but one more equal?

"Sanctity of life" a cliché?

the flowers of the supernatural and natural orders.

Syke: I am suspicious not of life but of pro-lifers. I have yet to meet a so-called pro-lifer who has compassion on real people. And I didn't meet one today either. I think you have to choose: either you love people more than principles, or principles more than people.

Loving principles vs. loving people

Socrates: That sounds like saying you must choose either to love numbers more than mathematics or mathematics more than numbers. What are true principles but the right ways of loving people?

Syke: Well, I have never met anyone who loved both principles and people totally and without compromise.

Socrates: What a shame; you have never met a saint.

Syke: Saints! Figments of legend and wishful thinking! Name a real, living saint for me, please.

Socrates: Mother Theresa, for one.

Syke: Name another.

Socrates: Melvin Schwarz.

Syke: Who's he?

Socrates: A saint.

Syke: I never heard of him.

Socrates: From that fact it does not logically follow that he is not a saint, unless you are God. Which perhaps you subconsciously think you are, since you arrogate to yourself the power of life and death over people—fetal people, at any rate. Would you like to talk about this divinity complex of yours and get in touch with your true feelings about it?

Abortion as playing God

Syke: I hope I'm interpreting your smile correctly, Socrates. You *are* kidding, aren't you?

Socrates: There is a kind of kidding that is quite serious, you know.

Syke: Why do you do this, Socrates?

Socrates: Because I serve a master.

Syke: How cruel he is! And how male, by the way!

Socrates: Ah, but he himself is a servant of a goddess called Sophia, Lady Wisdom.

Syke: Socrates, you are superstitious as well as rationalistic. The one thing you aren't is compassionate. In fact, you are the first person I ever met who got me to abandon my own method of compassion and positive reinforcement and stroking. I have degenerated into rationalizing and labeling, like you.

Socrates: So I am more of a threat to you than those murderers on death row that you worked with so successfully.

Syke: Indeed you are. For you show me not the heat of misdirected passion, which could be redirected by therapy, but cold logic, neither passion nor compassion. I'll bet you have no feelings even for poor girls who have just lost their dignity and their freedom and their control of their own lives by being raped. I'll bet you would refuse an abortion even to a rape victim, wouldn't you?

Socrates: I would refuse it, yes.

Syke: Do you realize how terrible her situation can be? Do you know how many rape victims go through life with permanent psychological scars? Do you know how many think of suicide? Do you know how many have great difficulties ever trusting a man again and making a happy marriage?

Abortion for rape victims?

Socrates: I do know something of this, yes. But I wonder whether you know something worse (since we are looking at terrible things now). Do you know how many abortion victims go through life, scarred or unscarred? None. Do you know how many would love to be born and never think of suicide? Do you know how many have great difficulties ever trusting a mother who kills them?

Syke: That's rhetoric, Socrates.

Socrates: Is it rhetoric to be cut into pieces or poisoned by burning acid or suctioned limb from limb into pieces?

Syke: You keep focusing on the fetus. Where is your compassion for the victimized mother?

Socrates: Because I have compassion for all, I don't want to see anyone victimized by anyone: fetus by mother *or* rape victim by rapist. But two wrongs don't make a right. Can you show me any other case where you would say it is right to answer the problem of being victimized by turning around and victimizing another person?

Two wrongs don't make a right.

Syke: Another *person,* no. You keep treating the fetus as a person.

Socrates: Because the argument forces me to. And once again we are back to our beginning.

Syke: Socrates, arguments are safe abstractions. But real people are quite different. They need compassion. It's easy to love words and principles and slogans, but it's costly to love real people.

Socrates: I agree.

Syke: I wonder. You seem to love words more than people. We've been squinting at words all afternoon here instead of getting in touch with people: ourselves, to begin with. I didn't have a chance to really dig into your psyche, we were so busy squinting at words.

Socrates: You think we were only looking at words?

Syke: Yes.

Socrates: I thought we were looking *through* them at

real people: mothers and fetuses. At least I was. Words seem to me like eyeglasses. I was looking through them; I hope you were not looking only at them. If so, no wonder our arguments did not meet. We each had a different focus.

Syke: Whatever the reason, we got nowhere with your method of verbalism. Each time the argument came back to the beginning, the first day.

Socrates: I think good arguments eventually always do that, if they follow the master, for he is both alpha and omega. Fortunately for us, we are not yet at omega, not yet finished, as an aborted fetus is—an aborted alpha, some may call it. For our successful passage through the perilous stage of our alpha, I think we should give thanks to that greatest class of unsung heroes of the human race, our mothers.

Syke: Sounds like you're divinizing motherhood.

Socrates: I believe motherhood is an image of God, at least. For God, it seems to me, is both our Father and our Mother.

Syke: Well, perhaps some other day we can talk about God.

Socrates: Perhaps. Unfortunately, some other day is never today, never real. The present of life is presented to us only in the present. I think there is a deep connection between the refusal of life and the refusal of the present...

Syke: Some other time, Socrates. I really must go. It's getting late.

Socrates: Indeed it is. Darkness falls quickly in December. But the sun will return. Of that, at least, we can be sure.

Syke: Good-bye, Socrates.

Socrates: God be with you, my friend.

Looking at words is looking through them.

Alpha and omega

Motherhood as image of God